MW01013321

No dles

Chinese Home – Cooking 家常篇

作　　　　者　　林麗華
出　版　　者　　純青出版社有限公司
　　　　　　　　台北市松江路125號5樓
　　　　　　　　郵政劃撥12106299
　　　　　　　　電話：(02)5074902 . 5084331
著作財產權人　　財團法人味全文化教育基金會
印　　　　刷　　中華彩色印刷股份有限公司

Author　　　　　Lee Hwa Lin
Publisher　　　　Chin Chin Publishing Co., Ltd.
　　　　　　　　5th fl., 125, Sung Chiang Rd,
　　　　　　　　Taipei, Taiwan, R.O.C.
　　　　　　　　TEL:(02)5074902 . 5084331
Copyright Holder　Wei-Chuan Cultural-Educational Foundation
Printer　　　　　China Color Printing Co., Inc.
Distributor　　　Wei-Chuan　Publishing
　　　　　　　　1455 Monterey Pass Rd, #110
　　　　　　　　Monterey Park, CA 91754, U.S.A.
　　　　　　　　TEL:(213)2613880 . 2613878
Printed in Taiwan, R.O.C.

序

麵,雖然是中國人的主食之一,但是經過各省不同的調理手法,呈現出千變萬化的風味,從麵、乾麵、撈麵、拉麵到刀削麵、貓耳朵……,都是以簡單的麵粉所製作出來的,而這本「家常麵」就將展示其中秘訣,並給您觸類旁通的概念。

現代人行止匆忙,對於家常小吃多著重營養,但是如何以簡單的烹飪技巧,調理出符合健康、美味的食品,是現代人極力追尋的;而麵食「家常篇」即針對這項需求,彙總了大江南北九十一道麵點,它不但是小家庭的必備手冊,單身貴族也相當適用。

為了編輯此書,味全文教基金會以一年的時間集結中國各省的麵食口味,並經過專業研發、考究,務求抓住地方特色與風味。除此之外,本書的另一特色是家常材料變化不同的麵點,讓讀者在掌握其中訣竅後,信手拈來都能烹調出讓人心滿意足的好麵點。

Noodle is one of the Chinese common staples. Due to differences of regional culture, noodle dishes present large varieties in tastes and cooking. From market sold dried noodle to home made shaved noodle or cat's ears, all are made from flour. This book, offers the basics of noodle cooking, and give readers an analogical concept to develop.

With hectic schedules, present modern family cooking mostly emphasizes nutrition. How to make nutritious and tasty food, using simple methods and in shortest time, has become the pursuit for modern families. With this urgent need in mind, this book collects 91 course of Chinese regional noodle dishes for this purpose. It is not only meant for families, but also a necessity for singles.

Wei-Chuan Cultural-Education Foundation, with more than one year's research and efforts, gathered all regional recipes and developed into easy recipes, yet still retaining its original flavors.At the same times, this book creates various noodle dishes with ordinary home materials; bringing readers a key to create your own noodle dishes with satisfactory results.

Lee Hwa Lin

目錄

麵體製作 · *Methods of Noodle Making*

麵的煮法 · *Guide to Noodle Cooking Methods*

材料的前處理 · *Preparation of Special Food Materials*

烹調的方法 · *Guide to Cooking Terms*

各種麵體的說明與換算 ....*General Information on Noodle Weight Equivalent Chart*

湯麵 · *Soup Noodle*

Contents

炒麵 · *Fried Noodle*

燴羹麵 • *Potagé and Sauce Noodle*

乾拌麵 • *Mixed Noodle*

涼麵 • *Cold Noodle*

重量換算表 • *Measurement Equivalents*

1磅 = 454公克 = 16盎士   1lb.= 454gm (454g.) = 16oz.

1盎士 = 28.4公克   1oz. = 28.4gm (28.4g.)

量器說明 • *Table of Measurements*

1杯 = 236c.c. = 1 cup (1C.)

1大匙 = 1湯匙 = 15c.c. = 1 Tablespoon (1T.)

1小匙 = 1茶匙 = 5c.c. = 1 Teaspoon (1t.)

麵體製作 • *Methods of Noodle Making*

雞蛋麵 • *Egg Noodle*

低筋麵粉 ------- ３００公克
高筋麵粉 ------- １００公克
雞蛋 -------------------- 3個
太白粉 ------------------ 適量

1 ⎰ 水 ----------- ４０公克
   ⎱ 鹽 ------------- ½小匙

300g.(10½oz.) ----- low gluten flour
100g.(3½oz.) ------ high gluten flour
3 -------------------- eggs
as needed - corn starch

1 ⎰ •40g.(1²/₅oz.)water
   ⎱ •½t.salt

1

2

3

1 將麵粉過篩，置於容器內，入雞蛋和 **1** 料拌勻，拌勻後揉成均勻且光滑之麵糰，再蓋上擰乾的濕布巾，醒３０分鐘。

2 將麵糰分成兩份，桌上撒上太白粉，把麵糰分別擀成２０公分×３０公分之麵皮後，在麵皮上撒些太白粉，再用擀麵棍捲起反覆壓平，使麵皮擀成０．１５～０．２公分厚的薄皮。

3 把擀好之麵皮折三摺，用刀切成０．２公分寬之細條，並撒上太白粉即可。

1 Sift flours and place in a large bowl. Add in eggs and **1** ; mix well with the flours and knead into a smooth dough. Cover with a damp towel and let it stand for 30 minutes.

2 Part the dough to two. Dust the table with corn starch and roll the dough into two 20 x 30 cm large sheets. Dust corn starch on the sheets, roll again and again with rolling pin until became 0.15 cm to 0.2 cm thin dough sheets.

3 Fold the sheets three times, and cut into 0.2 cm wide thin noodles. Dust on more corn starch to avoid sticking.

菠菜麵 • *Spinach Noodle*

低筋麵粉 ------- 250公克	250g.(8⁴/₅oz.) ------ low gluten flour
高筋麵粉 ------- 150公克	150g.(5¹/₃oz.) ------ high gluten flour
菠菜 ------------ 100公克	100g.(3¹/₂oz.) -- spinach
鹽 ---------------------- ½小匙	½t. -------------------- salt
太白粉 ------------------ 適量	as needed - corn starch

1   2

3

1 菠菜去頭洗淨,切成2公分長段,加200公克水用果汁機打成汁狀,再用濾網過濾去渣,汁液備用。

2 將麵粉及鹽過篩,置於容器內,入菠菜汁拌勻,再揉成均勻且光滑的麵糰,蓋上擰乾的濕布巾,醒10~20分鐘。

3 在桌上撲上少許的太白粉,把麵糰切成兩份後,分別擀成0‧2公分厚之大薄片,在麵皮上再撒少許的太白粉,折疊數層,切成0‧3公分寬之條狀即可。

■ 麵體之寬窄可依個人之喜好而定。

1 Wash spinach clean and trim off root; cut into 2 cm long sections. Add 200g.(7oz.) water and puree in juicer; sieve and discard dregs to be clear spinach juice.

2 Sift flour and salt, place into a large bowl; add in spinach juice and mix well, knead evenly into a smooth dough. Cover with damp cloth and let it stand for 10 - 20 minutes.

3 Dust a little corn starch on the working table, divide dough into two parts. Roll each into 0.2 cm thick large sheet. Dust again with a little corn starch. Fold into few layers and cut into 0.3 cm wide noodles.

■ The width of the noodle depends on personal.

麵片 • *Noodle Pieces*

中筋麵粉 ------- ４００公克　　400g.(14oz.) -------- all-
　　　　　　　　　　　　　　 purpose flour

1

2

1 麵粉過篩，置於容器內，加水２２５公克拌勻後揉成均勻且
光滑之麵糰，再將麵糰搓成直徑約３公分之長條，入冷水泡
２０分鐘，以增加麵糰之延展性。
2 清水入鍋煮開，取出麵糰以手拉成小薄片，入滾水中煮熟撈
起即可。

1 Sift flour and place into a large bowl, pour in
225g.(8oz.) water. Mix well and then knead into
a even and smooth dough. Then knead the dough
into 3 cm diameter strip. Soak in cold water for 20
minutes to increase its elasticity.
2 Boil water in a large pot. Pull thin noodle pieces
off the dough by hand. Cook in boiling water
until done.

刀切麵 • *Handmade Noodle*

中筋麵粉 ------- ４００公克　　400g.(14oz.) -------- all-
　　　　　　　　　　　　　　 purpose flour

1┌ 水 --------- ２００公克　　**1**┌ •200g.(7oz.) water
　└ 鹽 --------------- ½小匙　　　└ •½t.salt

1

2

1 麵粉過篩，置於容器內，入**1**料拌勻，拌勻後揉成均勻且光
滑之麵糰，蓋上擰乾的濕布巾，醒１０～２０分鐘，取出麵
糰置於已撒上乾麵粉的桌面上，再撒些乾粉於麵糰，用擀麵
棍壓成０‧２公分厚之大薄片。
2 麵皮上再撒些乾麵粉，摺數摺後切成０‧５公分寬之麵條即
可。
■ 喜食麵體較Q者，揉麵時水可少放些，喜食麵體較軟者，揉
麵時水可多放些。麵條之寬窄亦可依個人之喜好，切粗或切
細。

1 Sift flour and place into a large bowl; pour in **1**
and mix well. Then knead to a even and smooth
dough. Cover with damp cloth and let it stand for
10 - 20 minutes. Dust some flour on a working
table and the dough, roll the dough with rolling
pin into a 0.2 cm thick large sheet.
2 Dust the sheet with some flour again and fold into
few layers; then cut into 0.5 cm wide noodles.
■ If harder noodle desired, water may be reduced.
Therefore, water may be increased if softer noodle
favored. The width of the noodle also depends on
personal taste; may be cut wider or narrower.

刀削麵 • *Shaved Noodle*

中筋麵粉 ------- 4 0 0公克

1［ 水 --------- 1 8 0公克
　　 鹽 ---------------- ½小匙

400g.(14oz.) -------- all-purpose flour

1［ •180g. (5⅓oz.) water
　　 •½t.salt

1　2

1 麵粉過篩，置於容器內，入 **1** 料拌勻，拌勻後揉成較硬且光滑之麵糰，再壓成１５～１８公分長之圓筒狀。

2 清水置鍋內煮沸，一手托著麵糰，一手持刀將麵削成長１２～１５公分、寬１公分、厚０・１～０・３公分的麵條，下鍋煮熟，撈起瀝乾水分即可。

1 Sift flour and place in a large bowl; pour in **1** and mix well. Knead until it turns into a hard and smooth dough; press it into a 15 - 18 cm long cylinder shape.

2 Bring water to boil in a large pot. Hold the dough with one hand, and the other hand shave the dough with a knife into 12 - 15 cm long, 1 cm wide, and 0.1 - 0.3 cm thick noodle. Boil in water until cooked. Lift out and drain.

貓耳朵 • *Cat's Ears*

中筋麵粉 ------- 4 0 0公克

1［ 熱水（8 0℃）--------
　　 ------------ 2 0 0公克
　　 鹽 ---------------- ½小匙

400g.(11¼oz.) ------ all-purpose flour

1［ •200g.(6oz.) warm water(176°F or 80°C)
　　 •½t.salt

1

1 麵粉過篩，置於容器內，邊入 **1** 料邊用筷子拌勻，拌勻後揉成光滑的麵糰。

2 麵糰搓成直徑０・７公分寬之條狀，再切成０・５～１・０公克之小麵粒。

3 將麵粒置於工作檯上，用大姆指輕壓麵粒再拉捏，使麵粒成扁薄而微捲像貓耳朵的形狀即可。（為避免壓好之麵粒黏在一起，則撒些乾粉使之分開。）

2　3

1 Sift flour and place into a large bowl, pour in **1** and mix well with chopsticks. Then knead into a smooth dough.

2 Knead the dough into a 0.7 cm diameter wide strip; then cut into 0.5 - 1.0 g. small pieces.

3 Place dough pieces on a working table, press down on each piece with thumb and pull the sides out gently to resemble a cat's ear. (Dust with flour to avoid sticking.)

冷水煮麵 • *Boil Noodle*

1 １０杯水入鍋，加½小匙鹽煮開，入麵條並用筷子攪散。
2 待麵煮開後，續入１杯冷水煮至大滾，待麵心熟透，撈起瀝乾，放入煮好之湯料內即為湯麵。
3 若作為炒麵，則把煮熟之麵條撈起用冷水沖涼後，再瀝乾入鍋內與炒料同炒即可。
4 若作為涼拌類，其做法有二：
4-❶ 將煮熟之麵條撈起淋上少許麻油，拌勻後把麵置於通風處吹涼，再拌上作料即可。
4-❷ 將煮熟之麵條撈起用冷開水沖涼後，淋上作料拌勻即可。
■若麵條較寬，則第二次加水要多些且煮開後再滾約２分鐘使麵心熟透，若用乾麵條時，則煮的時間需再延長３～６分鐘。(視麵條之寬窄而定)

1 Bring 10C. water and ½t. salt to boil; add in noodle and loosen with chopsticks.
2 When noodle boiled, add in 1C. cold water; bring to boil again. When the center of noodle is cooked, remove and drain. Place noodle in soup to be soup noodle.
3 For fried noodle, rinse boiled noodle under cold water to cool; drain and fry with desired materials.
4 For cold and mixed noodle :
4-❶ Sprinkle boiled noodle with some sesame oil and mix well, place near a drafty spot to cool. Mix with desired sauce and serve.
4-❷ Rinse boiled noodle under cold water to cool, drain. Pour desired sauce over and mix well.
■When boil wider noodle, add cold water twice; after the second boil, let it boil 2 minutes more to ensure the center of the noodle is thoroughly cooked. If dried noodle used, then the boiling time should even be 3 - 6 minutes longer (Depends on the width of the noodle.)

1

2

3

4

油麵煮法 • *Boil Yellow Noodle*

1 生油麵煮法：10杯水加½小匙的鹽煮開，入生油麵並用筷子攪散，水開後，加1杯水，續煮至大滾，待麵心熟透，隨即撈起，用冷開水沖涼，瀝乾水分，拌上少許的沙拉油即可。

2 熟油麵煮法：若買回來即為煮熟的油麵，則食前再入開水中川燙一下或直接拿來炒 麵即可。（圖**2**中：① 為生油麵，② 為熟油麵。）

1 Fresh yellow noodle: Bring 10C. water and ½t. salt to boil, add in noodle and loosen with chopsticks. After water boil again, add in 1C. cold water; bring to boil again. When the center of the noodle is thoroughly cooked, remove and drain. Rinse under cold water, drain, and mix with some salad oil.

2 Boiled yellow noodle: (Market sold yellow noodle ususally is already boiled.) Scald in boiling water before serving or directly use it for fried noodle. (illus. **2**, ① fresh yellow noodle. ② boiled yellow noodle.)

2

麵線煮法 • *Boil Noodle String*

1 淡味麵線煮法除不加鹽外其餘做法與冷水煮麵相同。

2 若為鹹味麵線，則鍋內入12杯水，煮開後入麵線，其餘做法與冷水煮麵相同。（圖**2**中：①為淡味黑麵線，②為淡味白麵線，③ 為鹹味白麵線。）

1 For unsalted noodle string, the method remains the same as boiled noodle except no salt added.

2 For salted noodle string, bring 12C. water to boil; add in noodle string. The rest remains the same as boiled noodle. (illus. **2**, ① unsalted black noodle string. ② unsalted white noodle string. ③ salted white noodle string.)

1

2

炸麵 • *Deep Fried Noodle*

1 將陽春麵入沸水中並用筷子攪散煮片刻（約1分鐘），撈起瀝乾。

2 油3杯燒至160℃，入麵條炸，炸至一邊堅硬且呈金黃色時翻面炸，再炸至麵條兩面皆呈金黃色時，撈起瀝乾即可。

1 Drop noodle into boiling water and loosen with chopsticks (about 1 minute). Remove and drain.

2 Heat 3C. oil to 160℃ (320°F), fry noodle until hard and golden on one side. Turn and fry the other side. Remove and drain on paper towel.

1   2

伊麵 • *E-Fu Noodle*

1 使用雞蛋麵，其做法同炸麵。

1 Egg noodle is used. Deep fry egg noodle as above to make e-fu noodle.

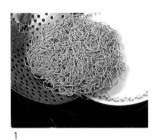

1

兩面黃 • *Noodle Pancake*

1 將麵條入沸水中並用筷子攪散煮片刻（約10秒），續入1杯冷水煮至大滾，撈起瀝乾，加少許沙拉油、醬油、麻油拌勻備用。

2 平底鍋燒熱入2大匙的沙拉油，把**1**項之麵條入鍋煎，並不時搖動鍋子，避免黏鍋，再逐次添加少許的沙拉油，用中火煎至麵條兩面呈金黃色且香脆即可。

■ 兩面黃可用陽春麵或雞蛋麵製作，但以雞蛋麵的效果較佳。

1 Drop noodle into boiling water and loosen with chopsticks (about 10 seconds), add in 1C. cold water and bring to boil again. Remove and drain. Mix in some salad oil, soy sauce, and sesame oil.

2 Heat a skillet, add 2T. oil; fry **1** noodle. Shake the skillet constantly to avoid sticking. Add in a little more oil during frying if needed. Fry over medinum heat until golden on both sides.

■ Noodle pancake may be made from plain noodle or egg noodle, but egg noodle usually results the best.

1

2

材料的前處理 · *Preparation of Special Food Materials*

花枝的處理 · *Squid*

1 花枝去皮、頸。
2 去除內臟,並用水洗淨。
3 花枝肉之內面,每隔0‧3公分縱橫切入⅓深度,使肉身作
交叉片狀。
4 將片狀花枝切成4公分寬之條狀。
5 每一條花枝肉再切成4×5公分之片狀。

1 Discard the neck and peel off the skin.
2 Discard the inner gut and wash clean.
3 Score inner surface lengthwise and crosswise
every 0.3 cm and ⅓ deep into the flesh.
4 Cut into 4 cm wide large strips.
5 Then cut each strip into 4 x 5 cm serving pieces.

1

2

3

4

5

海參的發法 · *Dried Sea Cucumber*

1 乾海參洗淨,泡水一天,隔天換水煮開,煮開後熄火浸泡,
待水涼再換水煮開,熄火浸泡,如此一天3次,連續發兩天
至軟。
2 由腹部剪開,取出內臟洗淨,加水煮開,再發一天即可。
3 若買發好之海參,則剪開肚子取出內臟洗淨即可。

1 Wash the dried sea cucumber clean, soak in water
for one day. Place sea cucumber into new clean
water and bring to boil; turn off the heat and soak
until water cools. Change again to new clean
water and bring to boil; turn off the heat and
continue soaking until water cools. Repeat the
process 3 times a day for 2 days until sea
cucumber softened.
2 Snip open lengthwise and clean out the intestines.
Cover with water and bring to boil. Remove from
heat and let it stand for one more day. Then it is
ready for cooking.
3 Already soaked sea cucumber can also be bought,
then only need to snip open lengthwise and clean
out the intestines.

1

2

3

蝦仁清洗方法 • *Shrimp*

1 蝦仁用牙籤由背面挑去腸泥（若帶殼，則先去殼）。
2 加太白粉、鹽、輕輕拌勻。
3 用清水洗淨，瀝乾。

1 Devine the shrimp with toothpick (must be shelled first).
2 Clean shrimp by rubbing gently with corn starch and salt.
3 Rinse under water and drian.

1　2

3

海蜇皮的處理 • *Jelly Fish*

1 海蜇皮先洗淨，切絲泡冷水，泡水時需不斷換水，以去鹹味。
2 海蜇皮入半滾水中川燙，隨即撈出，再浸泡冷水至柔軟即可使用。

1 Wash jelly fish clean, shred and soak in water. Change water often to rid of the salty taste.
2 Scald jelly fish in half-boiling water; lift out immediately. Soak in cold water again until softened.

1　2

牛筋的處理 • *Beef Tendon*

1 水一大鍋煮沸後，加少許的蔥、薑、酒、及牛筋煮約5小時至爛即可，過程中若有白色渣渣出現，則用杓子撈掉。
■ 若用壓力鍋煮則約需3小時。

1 Bring a large pot of water to boil, add a little green onion, ginger, cooking wine, and beef tendon in to simmer for 5 hours or until tender. Skim off the white foam during simmering.
■ If pressure cooker used, 3 hours will be sufficient.

1

薑泥和薑汁的製作 • *Ginger Paste and Ginger Juice*

1 薑洗淨，去皮。
2 用磨泥板磨成泥，即為薑泥，再過濾去渣即為薑汁。

1 Wash ginger clean and trim off skin.
2 Rub on a mash board to finely mashed ginger; It is
ginger paste. Sieve and discard the sediments to
be clear ginger juice.

1　2

蒜泥的製作 • *Garlic Paste*

1 蒜洗淨，去皮。
2 用磨泥板磨成泥即可。

1 Wash garlic clean, peel off skin.
2 Rub on a mash board to finely mashed garlic.

1　2

銀芽 • *Bean Sprout*

1 將綠豆芽之頭、尾去除，謂之銀芽。

1 Discard the bean tip and root.

1

筍的處理 • *Bamboo Shoot*

1 新鮮筍去殼，入水中煮至熟，再取出漂涼即可，若是罐頭
筍，有些因製罐關係，會帶有些微酸味，可以先入鍋川燙以
去酸味。

1 Peel off the hard shell; boil until cooked, drain and
cool.　If canned bamboo used, it will be slightly
sour; parboil in boiling water to rid of sour taste
before cooking.

1

蔥段的切法 • *Green Onion Sections*

1 蔥洗淨。
2 去頭、尾部分。
3 切成 3 公分長段。

1 Wash green onion clean.
2 Trim off the tops and roots.
3 Cut into 3 cm long sections.

1 2

3

洋菇的處理 • *Mushroom*

1 若新鮮洋菇則需先入開水中煮熟，再取出漂涼，即為熟洋菇。
2 若罐頭洋菇，則開罐後瀝乾水分，再用沸水漂過即可使用。

1 Fresh mushroom needs to be boiled first, then rinse under cold water.
2 If canned mushroom used, drain; and then rinse with boiling water.

1 2

番茄的處理 • *Tomato*

1 番茄洗淨，表面劃米字，入沸水中煮至皮開，撈起漂涼，瀝乾再去皮。
2 將番茄橫切，把籽去掉即可。

1 Wash tomato clean; score a cross on the surface. Place in boiling water until skin opens. Lift out and cool. Peel.
2 Cut tomato widthwise and discard the seeds.

1 2

烹調的方法 · *Guide to Cooking Terms*

上湯的製作 · *Consommé*

1 雞、豬、中式火腿的肉切成 3～4 公分之小塊，入沸水中川燙後取出洗淨。
2 以另一鍋水燒開再入洗淨的肉，並加少許胡椒粒、陳皮，慢火熬出來的湯，謂之上湯。

1 Cut chicken, pork, and Chinese ham into 3 - 4 cm cubes; parboil in boiling water. Lift out and rinse clean.
2 Bring a pot of water to boil, add in parboiled meats with a pinch of pepper corn and dried orange peel. Simmer over low heat until the consommé is tasty.

1

2

高湯的製作 · *Stock*

1 以豬、牛、雞的肉或骨入沸水中川燙。
2 再將肉或骨頭取出洗淨。
3 以另一鍋水燒開，再入洗淨的肉或骨頭，並加少許蔥、薑、酒，慢火熬出來的湯，謂之高湯。
■ 本書使用之高湯為依此法所製之高湯，若使用市售之高湯製作麵食，則需再降低鹽及味精的用量。

1 Parboil pork, beef, chicken or bones.
2 Lift out and rinse clean.
3 Bring new clean water to boil, add in meat or bones together with a little green onion, ginger, and cooking wine. Simmer over low heat until the stock is tasty.
■ If can broth is used, seasonings may be reduced.

1

2

3

煮出汁的製作 • *Seaweed Stock*

1 乾海帶（2公克）用布擦乾淨，剪成1公分寬之條狀。
2 鍋內入水兩杯及海帶，煮至快沸騰時取出海帶，續入柴魚片（10公克）並立即熄火，待柴魚片沈澱後過濾，此即為煮出汁。

1 Wipe dried seaweed (2g.) clean with a cloth; snip into 1 cm wide strips.
2 Add 2C. water and seaweed in a pot, cook until nearly to boiling point. Lift out seaweed, add in dried fish flakes (10g. or ⅓ oz.) and turn off heat immediately. When fish flakes sink to the bottom of the stock, sieve to be clear seaweed stock.

1   2

川燙 • *Parboil*

1 鍋水以大火煮沸。
2 放入材料再煮沸，隨即撈起。
3 漂冷水。

1 Bring water to boil over high heat.
2 Add in material and bring to boil once again. Quickly lift out.
3 Rinse under cold water.

1   2

3

過油 • *Hot Oil Soaking*

1 將食物泡入熱油內（五分熱120℃），食物剛熟即刻撈出，時間不可過長，謂之過油。

1 Soak material into semi-hot oil (248°F/120°C), lift out as soon as material is cooked. It should be done in a minimum time required.

1

各種麵體的說明與換算

1 自製生麵重：是指家庭手工所製成麵條之生重。
2 市售生乾麵：是市場所賣經過烘乾加工，麵體直而堅硬且包裝完整之生麵。
3 市售生濕麵：是市場所賣未經烘乾加工，麵體較軟且形狀無法固定之生麵。
4 市售熟麵：是指市場所賣經煮熟後再冷卻之熟麵條，如一般之油麵及烏龍麵等。
5 熟重：意指經本文所介紹麵的煮法煮熟之麵體重。
6 本食譜所指陽春麵即為市售之生白麵條。
7 日式素麵：即為市售之日本麵，其麵體色白且較陽春麵為細。
8 廈門麵線：與白麵線相似，只是麵體比較細。
9 以下所指麵體重皆以一人份為準。

麵體名稱	自製生麵重	市售生乾麵重	市售生濕麵重	市售熟麵重	熟重
1. 刀削麵	135公克				220公克
2. 刀切麵	150公克				220公克
3. 麵片	160公克				220公克
4. 雞蛋麵	150公克	90公克	120公克		220公克
5. 伊麵			100公克		90公克
6. 炸麵			100公克		90公克
7. 兩面黃			120公克		170公克
8. 貓耳朵	135公克				200公克
9. 菠菜麵	150公克	90公克			220公克
10. 陽春麵		90公克	120公克		220公克
11. 烏龍麵				220公克	
12. 油麵		90公克		200公克	200公克
13. 意麵			120公克		220公克
14. 黑麵線			70公克		190公克
15. 白麵線		75公克	90公克		220公克
16. 廈門麵線		75公克	90公克		220公克
17. 蕎麥麵		80公克	110公克		200公克
18. 拉麵		90公克	120公克		220公克
19. 日式素麵		80公克			220公克

General Information on Noodle Weight Equivalent Chart:

1 Weight of uncooked homemade fresh noodle: It means the weight of uncooked freshly homemade and usually handmade noodle.

2 Weight of uncooked dehydrated noodle: Uncooked dehydrated noodle is processed through dehydration. It is usually straight and hard, sold in manufacturer's packaging at market. This means the weight of raw noodle before cooking.

3 Weight of uncooked freshly made noodle: It applies to market sold fresh noodle which has not been processed. It is usually wet and soft, sometimes with no certain forms or shapes. This means the weight of the noodle before cooking.

4 Weight of ready-made noodle: It applies to market sold noodle which is ready cooked and cooled, such as yelllow noodle or udon. This means the weight of purchased amount.

5 Weight after cooking: This means the weight of the noodle after it is prepared according to cooking guidance of this book.

6 Plain noodle used in this cook book means market sold white, uncooked, fresh, round noodle of medium thickness.

7 Japanese So Mein: It means market sold Japanese noodle, It is whiter and thinner than plain noodle.

8 Amoy noodle string: It is similar to white noodle string, but even thinner.

9 All the weights indicated below is of one serving.

Name	Weight of un-cooked home-made noodle	Weight of un-cooked dehy-drated noodle	Weight of un-cooked freshly made noodle	Weight of ready-made noodle	Weight after cooking
1. Shaved noodle	135g.(4¾oz.)				220g.(7¾oz.)
2. Handmade noodle	150g.(5⅓oz.)				220g.(7¾oz.)
3. Noodle pieces	160g.(5⅗oz.)				220g.(7¾oz.)
4. Egg noodle	150g.(5⅓oz.)	90g.(3⅕oz.)	120g.(4¼oz.)		220g.(7¾oz.)
5. E-fu noodle			100g.(3½oz.)		90g.(3⅕oz.)
6. Deep fried noodle			100g.(3½oz.)		90g.(3⅕oz.)
7. Noodle pancake			120g.(4¼oz.)		170g.(6oz.)
8. Cat's ears	135g.(4¾oz.)				200g.(7oz.)
9. Spinach noodle	150g.(5⅓oz.)	90g.(3⅕oz.)			220g.(7¾oz.)
10. Plain noodle		90g.(3⅕oz.)	120g.(4¼oz.)		220g.(7¾oz.)
11. Udon				220g.(7¾oz.)	
12. Yellow noodle		90g.(3⅕oz.)		200g.(7oz.)	200g.(7oz.)
13. Yi-mein			120g.(4¼oz.)		220g.(7¾oz.)
14. Black noodle string			70g.(2½oz.)		190g.(6⅔oz.)
15. White noodle string		75g.(2⅔oz.)	90g.(3⅕oz.)		220g.(7¾oz.)
16. Amoy noodle string		75g.(2⅔oz.)	90g.(3⅕oz.)		220g.(7¾oz.)
17. Buckwheat noodle		80g.(2⅘oz.)	110g.(4oz.)		200g.(7oz.)
18. Hand-pulled noodle		90g.(3⅕oz.)	120g.(4¼oz.)		220g.(7¾oz.)
19. Japanese So Mein		80g.(2⅘oz.)			220g.(7¾oz.)

鍋燒烏龍麵

•Udon in Pot

四人份　serve　4

鍋燒烏龍麵 • *Udon in Pot*

烏龍麵	-------------	8 8 0公克
蛤蜊	-------------	1 8 0公克
雞胸肉	-------------	1 6 0公克
菠菜	-------------	1 2 0公克
魚丸	-------------	4 0公克
香菇	-------------	8 公克
高湯	-------------	9 杯
劍蝦	-------------	8 隻
蛋	-------------	4 個
魚板	-------------	½條

1
┌ 蛋白 ------------- 1 小匙
│ 酒、麻油、太白粉 --------
│ ------------- 各½小匙
│ 鹽 ------------- ¼小匙
└ 胡椒粉 ------------- ⅛小匙

3
┌ 麻油 ------------- 1 大匙
│ 鹽、味醂 ------- 各 1 小匙
│ 酒、味精 ------- 各½小匙
└ 胡椒粉 ------------- ⅛小匙

2
┌ 蠔油 ------------- 1 小匙
└ 糖、醬油 --------- 各½小匙

1 雞胸肉切5×3公分薄片，以 **1** 料醃30分鐘，蛤蜊泡水吐沙，劍蝦去腸泥，魚丸切半，魚板切薄片備用。

2 菠菜入開水中川燙後，撈起瀝乾切3公分段備用。

3 香菇泡軟去蒂加高湯及 **2** 料煮至入味（約8分鐘）後，入烏龍麵、魚丸、魚板煮開，再入蝦、蛤蜊及 **3** 料，以大火煮開，再將雞胸肉一片片放入煮開，最後再加蛋煮至半固體狀時，熄火，放入菠菜即可。

■ 食用時可加辣椒粉及蔥末，以增加風味。

880g.(2lb.)	--udon
180g.(6⅓oz.)	--clam
160g.(5⅗oz.)	--------------------------------chicken breast
120g.(4¼oz.)	--------------------------------------spinach
40g.(1⅖oz.)	--fish ball
8g.(¼oz.)	----------------------------dried black mushroom
9C.	--stock
8	--shrimp
4	--eggs
½ block	--kamaboko

1
┌ •1t.egg white
│ •½t.each cooking wine, sesame oil,corn starch
│ •¼t.salt
└ •⅛t.pepper

2
┌ •1t.oyster sauce
└ •½t.each sugar, soy sauce

3
┌ •1T.sesame oil
│ •1t.each salt, mirin
│ •½t.cooking wine
└ •⅛t.pepper

1 Cut chicken breast into 5 x 3 cm thin slices, marinate with **1** for 30 minutes. Soak clam in water to rid sand; de-vein shrimp; cut fish balls to halves; slice kamaboko thin.

2 Parboil spinach in boiling water, drain and cut into 3 cm serving sections.

3 Soften mushroom in warm water and discard stem. Add mushroom in stock and **2** , boil until tasty (about 8 minutes); add in udon, fish ball, and kamaboko, bring to boil. Add in shrimp, clam, and **3**, bring to boil over high heat, add in chicken slice by slice; boil again. Then add in eggs on top, cook until half set. Turn off heat and add in spinach. Serve directly from the pot.

■Chili powder and minced green onion can be sprinkled on top to enhance the flavor.

海鮮鍋燒麵 · *Seafood Udon in Pot*

烏龍麵 ------------- ８８０公克	生蠔 ----------------- ８０公克
大白菜、蒜苗 ---各２００公克	劍蝦、鮮干貝 ------各６０公克
花枝淨重 ----------- １８０公克	魚板 --------------------------¼條
海參 --------------- １４０公克	高湯 ------------------------- ９杯

1	醬油 ---------------- 1 大匙
	鹽、麻油、酒 --各 2 小匙
	糖 ------------------ 1 小匙
	味精 --------------- ½小匙
	胡椒粉 ------------- ¼小匙

1 劍蝦剪去鬚腳、去腸泥，花枝切３×４公分花刀，干貝切片，海
參洗淨切滾刀塊，大白菜切４×５公分塊狀，蒜苗切斜薄片，蒜
白、蒜葉分開，魚板切片備用。

2 鍋熱入油４大匙燒熱，將蒜白炒香，續入白菜炒軟，移入鍋中，
入高湯煮開後，續入烏龍麵待滾，再入花枝、海參、劍蝦及 **1** 料
煮開，最後入干貝、生蠔、魚板再煮開並灑上蒜葉即可。

880g.(2lb.) ---------- udon	80g.(2⁴/₅oz) ---------- oyster
200g.(7oz.)each ---- garlic leek, Chinese cabbage	60g.(2¹/₉oz.)each - shrimp, scallop
180g.(6¹/₃oz.) --- squid (net weight)	¼block --------- kamaboko
140g.(5oz.) sea cucumber	9C. -------------------- stock

1	• 1T.soy sauce
	• 2t.each sesame oil, salt , cooking wine
	• 1t.sugar
	• ¼t.pepper

1 De-vein shrimp, snip off legs and antenna. Cut squid
into 3 x 4 cm slanting pieces. Slice scallop. Wash sea
cucumber clean and cut into diamond cubes. Cut
cabbage into 4 x 5 cm pieces. Slice garlic leek thin,
and separate white and green parts. Slice kamaboko.

2 Heat the wok, add 4T. oil and heat to hot; stir fry
garlic leek white until fragrant. Add in cabbage, stir
fry until softened. Remove into a pot, pour in stock
and bring to boil. Add in udon, boil again. Add in
squid, sea cucumber, shrimp and **1**; bring to boil
again. Then add in scallop, oyster and kamaboko;
bring to boil. Sprinkle on garlic leek green and serve.

三鮮湯麵 • *Seafood Noodle*

熟陽春麵 ----------- ８８０公克	瘦肉、熟洋菇片 --- 各６０公克	
墨魚 ---------------- ３００公克	高湯 --------------------- ８杯	
小白菜 ------------- １６０公克	蔥段 --------------------- ５段	
海參、劍蝦 ------ 各１４０公克		

1
- 水 ------------------- 1 杯
- 薑片 ------------------ 1 片
- 酒 --------------------- ½大匙

3
- 醬油 ----------------- 1 大匙
- 酒、麻油 ------ 各 1 ½小匙
- 鹽 ------------------- 1 小匙
- 味精、烏醋 ------ 各½小匙
- 胡椒粉 --------------- ⅛小匙

2
- 太白粉 -------------- ¼小匙
- 鹽、胡椒粉 ------ 各⅛小匙

1　小白菜洗淨切段，海參去內臟洗淨切滾刀塊，入**1**料川燙撈起，劍蝦去腸泥洗淨，墨魚洗淨切花刀條狀。
2　瘦肉切絲以**2**料醃約３０分鐘，鍋熱入油４杯燒至六分熱（約１４０℃），入肉絲及墨魚過油撈起。
3　鍋內留油２大匙燒熱，入蔥段、洋菇、劍蝦略炒，續入高湯煮開並以**3**料調味，再入小白菜、海參、墨魚、肉絲煮開即為麵湯。
4　麵條置於碗中，淋上麵湯即可。

■三鮮烏龍麵：將熟陽春麵改為烏龍麵，其餘材料及做法同三鮮湯麵。

880g.(2lb.) ---------- boiled plain noodle	140g.(5oz.)each ------- sea cucumber, shrimp	
300g.(10½oz.) ------- squid	60g.(2⅑oz.)each ----- lean pork, canned mushroom slices	
160g.(5⅗oz.) --------- baby cabbage		
8C. -------------------- stock	5 sections ---- green onion	

1
- •1C.water
- •1 slice ginger
- •½T.cooking wine

3
- •1T.soy sauce
- •1½t. each cooking wine, sesame oil
- •1t.salt
- •½t.brown vinegar
- •⅛t.pepper

2
- •¼t .corn starch
- •⅛t.each salt, pepper

1　Wash clean sea cucumber and discard entrails, cut into slanting serving pieces. Parboil in **1**. De-vein shrimp; clean squid and cut into serving strips.
2　Shred pork and marinate in **2** for 30 minutes. Heat the wok, add 4C. oil and heat to 140℃ (280°F); soak pork and squid in hot oil, lift out immediately.
3　Keep 2T. oil in the wok and heat to hot; stir fry green onion, mushroom and shrimp, add in stock and bring to boil, season with **3**. Then add in cabbage, sea cucumber, squid, and pork; bring to boil to be the noodle soup.
4　Place noodle in individual bowls, pour soup over and serve.

■ Seafood Udon : Replace boiled plain noodle with Udon. The rest of materials and methods are the same as above.

四人份　serve 4

紅燒牛肉麵 • *Beef Stew Soup Noodle*

熟陽春麵	880公克	薑片	8片
牛腩	850公克	蔥末	2½大匙
小白菜	180公克	辣豆瓣醬、豆瓣醬	各1½大匙
蔥段	20段	蒜末	1大匙

❶
- 八角 ------------- 1顆
- 花椒粒 ----------- 1大匙
- 小茴 ------------- ½大匙
- 桂皮(拍碎) -------- ½小匙

❷
- 醬油 ------------- 3½大匙
- 糖色、酒 --------- 各1大匙
- 糖 --------------- 1小匙
- 味精 ------------- ⅓小匙
- 鹽 --------------- ¼小匙

1 牛腩洗淨川燙切成3公分小塊，小白菜洗淨切段燙熟，**❶**料以小布袋裝起來即為滷包。

2 燉鍋中放入牛腩、**❶**料及水10杯煮開，改小火燉約1½小時後，將牛腩及滷包撈起，牛肉汁留著備用。

3 另鍋熱入油4大匙，將蒜末、蔥段、薑片、豆瓣醬及辣豆瓣醬爆香，再入牛腩、滷包、**❷**料及牛肉汁5杯煮開後改小火燉煮15分鐘即為牛肉湯。

4 麵條置於碗中，上置小白菜並淋上牛肉湯，再灑上蔥末即可。

■ **紅燒牛肉刀削麵**：將熟陽春麵改為熟刀削麵，其餘材料及做法同紅燒牛肉麵。

880g.(2lb.)	boiled plain noodle	20 sections	green onion
850g.(1⅝lb.)	beef brisket	8 slices	ginger
180g.(5³/₅oz.)	baby cabbage	2½T.	minced green onion
		1½T.each	hot soy bean paste, soy bean paste
		1T.	minced garlic

❶
- 1 piece star anise
- 1T.Szechwan pepper corn
- ½T.fennel
- ½t.crushed cinnamon

❷
- 3½T.soy sauce
- 1T. each sugar coloring, cooking wine
- 1t.sugar
- ¼t.salt

1 Wash beef clean, parboil in boiling water, and cut into 3 cm cubes. Wash baby cabbage clean and cut into serving sections, boil in boiling water until cooked. Put all spices of **❶** into a small cloth bag.

2 In a large pot, put in beef, **❶**, and 10C. water; bring to boil. Turn heat to low and simmer for 1½ hours. Lift out the beef and spice bag. Keep beef juice for later use.

3 Heat the wok, add 4T. oil and heat to hot; stir fry garlic, ginger slices, hot soy bean paste and soy bean paste until fragrant. Add in beef, spice bag, **❷**, and 5C. beef juice; bring to boil. Turn heat to low and simmer for 15 minutes to be beef soup.

4 Place noodle in individual bowls, arrange baby cabbage on top. Pour over beef soup, sprinkle on minced green onion and serve.

■ Beef Stew Soup Shaved Noodle : Replace boiled plain noodle with boiled shaved noodle. The rest of materials and methods are the same as above.

清燉牛肉麵 • *Clear Beef Soup Noodle*

熟陽春麵 ----------- 880公克	薑片 ------------------- 8片
牛腱 ----------------- 850公克	蔥末 ------------------- 3大匙
蔥段 ---------------------- 20段	花椒粒 ------------------- 1大匙

1〔 蔥段 ------------------- 8段
　 薑片 ------------------- 3片

2〔 酒 -------------------- 2大匙
　 鹽 -------------------- 1大匙
　 味精 ----------------- ¼小匙

1 將牛腱及 **1** 料入滾水中川燙後取出牛腱洗淨，花椒粒裝在小布袋中備用。

2 鍋熱入油3大匙燒熱，入蔥段、薑片爆香，續入水18杯、牛腱及花椒粒煮開後，改小火燜煮至牛肉熟爛（約3½小時），取出牛腱待涼切片，剩餘高湯過濾取湯汁，再加 **2** 料煮開即為牛肉湯。

3 麵條置於碗中，牛肉排於麵上，灑上蔥末並淋上牛肉湯即可。

■ 清燉牛肉刀削麵：將熟陽春麵改為熟刀削麵，其餘材料及做法同清燉牛肉麵。

■ 牛腱可以牛腩取代，喜好重口味者可以添加蒜末或辣椒末。

880g.(2lb.) --- boiled plain noodle	8 slices --------------- ginger
	3T. ---------- minced garlic
850g.(1⅘lb.) - beef shank	1T. Szechwan pepper corn
20 sections -- green onion	

1〔 •8 sections　green onion
　 •3 slices　ginger

2〔 •2T. cooking wine
　 •1t. salt

1 Scald beef and **1** in boiling water. Lift out and rinse clean. Put pepper corn in a small cloth bag, and tie up the opening.

2 Heat the wok, add 3T. oil and heat to hot; stir fry green onion sections and ginger until fragrant. Add in 18C. water, beef, and pepper corn, bring to boil. Turn heat to low and simmer until beef is tender(about 3½ hours); lift out and slice when cooled. Sieve the soup and discard dregs, season with **2** to be the beef soup.

3 Place noodle in individual bowls, arrange beef slices on top, sprinkle on minced green onion. Pour beef soup over and serve.

■ Clear Beef Soup Shaved Noodle : Replace boiled plain noodle with boiled shaved noodle. The rest of materials and methods are the same as above.

■ Beef shank may be replaced by beef brisket. Minced garlic or chili powder can be added for those prefer spicier taste.

Da-Lu Mein

大滷麵

四人份　serve　4

28

大滷麵 · *Da-Lu Mein*

熟陽春麵 ------------ ８８０公克
梅花肉 -------------- １８０公克
大白菜 -------------- １６０公克
熟筍 ---------------- １３０公克
鮑魚菇、濕木耳 ---- 各４０公克
乾金針 -------------- ３０公克
蝦米 ---------------- ２０公克
高湯 ------------------ ８杯
蛋 -------------------- ３個

1
太白粉 ------------ １大匙
醬油 ------------ ２小匙
麻油 ------------ １小匙

3
水 ------------ ４大匙
太白粉 ------------ ２大匙

2
醬油 ---------------- ２大匙
蒜末 ------------ １½大匙
麻油、烏醋 ------ 各１大匙
鹽 ------------------ １小匙
味精 ---------------- ¼小匙
胡椒粉 -------------- ⅛小匙

1 梅花肉切５×４公分薄片，以**1**料醃２０分鐘，大白菜、筍、鮑
魚菇、木耳去蒂，均切３×４公分片狀，金針泡軟去蒂打結，
蝦米洗淨切碎，蛋打散備用。

2 鍋熱入油３大匙燒熱，爆香蝦米，再將肉一片片入鍋，使之不要
重疊煎一下，再入大白菜、筍、鮑魚菇、木耳和金針炒勻後，續
入高湯及**2**料煮開，以**3**料勾芡，再加蛋液並淋上１大匙豬油
即為滷麵湯。

3 麵條置於碗中，淋上滷麵湯即可。

■ 大滷貓耳朵、大滷刀削麵：將熟陽春麵改為熟貓耳朵或熟刀削
麵，其餘材料及做法同大滷麵。

880g.(2lb.) ----------------------------- boiled plain noodle
180g.(6⅓oz.) ----------------------------- pork shoulder
160g.(5³/₅oz.) --------------------------- Chinese cabbage
130g.(4³/₅oz.) ------------------------ boiled bamboo shoot
40g.(1²/₅oz.)each ------------- abalone mushroom, soaked
black wood ear
30g.(1oz.) ------------------------------ dried lily bud
20g.(²/₃oz.) -------------------------- dried baby shrimp
8C. --- stock
3 --- eggs

1
•1T.corn starch
•2t.soy sauce
•1t.sesame oil

2
•2T.soy sauce
•1½T.minced garlic
•1T.each sesame oil, brown vinegar
•1t.salt
•⅛t.pepper

3
•4T.water
•2T.corn starch

1 Cut pork into 5 x 4 cm thin slices, marinate with **1** for
20 minutes. Discard stem from wood ear. Cut wood
ear, cabbage, bamboo, and abalone mushroom into
3 x 4 cm thin slices. Soften dried lily bud in warm
water, discard tough stem, and tie into knots. Wash
shrimp clean and chop fine. Beat eggs.

2 Heat the wok, add 3T. oil and heat to hot; stir fry
shrimp until fragrant. Add in pork to fry, slice by slice
in order not to stick together. Then add in cabbage,
bamboo, abalone mushroom, wood ear, and lily bud
to fry; mix well. Pour in stock and **2**, bring to boil.
Thicken with **3**, pour egg in and sprinkle on 1T. pork
lard to be da-lu potagé.

3 Place noodle in individual bowls, pour potagé over
and serve.

■ Da-Lu Cat's Ears and Da-Lu Shaved Noodle : Replace
boiled plain noodle with boiled cat's ears or boiled
shaved noodle. The rest of materials and methods are
the same as above.

排骨湯麵

·*Soup Noodle with Pork Chop*

四人份　**serve　4**

排骨湯麵 • *Soup Noodle with Pork Chop*

熟陽春麵	880公克
大排骨肉	480公克
高湯	8 杯
地瓜粉	1 杯
蔥末	5 大匙

1
蛋黃	1 個
蔥段	5 段
醬油	2 大匙
蒜末	1 大匙
糖	2 小匙
麻油、酒	各 1 ½小匙
太白粉、蠔油、烏醋	各 1 小匙
胡椒粉	½小匙
番茄醬、甜麵醬	各¼小匙

2
醬油	2 大匙
鹽	1 小匙
味精、胡椒粉	各½小匙

3
豬油	2 ½大匙
紅蔥頭	17公克

4
鹽	1 小匙
味精、胡椒粉	各¼小匙

1 大排骨肉切 1 公分厚，將肉邊緣之白筋切斷並略加拍鬆，入**1**料拌勻醃約 1 小時備用。

2 紅蔥頭洗淨切末，將豬油與紅蔥頭爆香成蔥油備用。

3 鍋熱入油 5 杯燒至八分熱（180℃），排骨肉沾地瓜粉入油鍋中炸至金黃色撈起，並灑上拌勻之 **4** 料，再切成 4 公分之長條狀。

4 高湯煮開，加入 **2**、**3**料調味即為麵湯。

5 麵條置於碗中，加入麵湯，再上置排骨及蔥末即可。

880g.(2lb.)	boiled plain noodle
480g.(1lb.)	pork loin with bone
8C.	stock
1C.	sweet potato flour
5T.	minced green onion

1
- 1 egg yolk
- 5 sections green onion
- 2T.soy sauce
- 1T.minced garlic
- 2t.sugar
- 1½t.each sesame oil, cooking wine
- 1t.each corn starch, oyster sauce, brown vinegar
- ½t.pepper
- ¼t.each catchup, sweet soy bean paste

2
- 2T.soy sauce
- 1t.salt
- ½t.pepper

3
- 2½T.pork lard
- 17g.(³/₅oz.) red shallot

4
- 1t.salt
- ¼t.pepper

1 Cut pork to 1 cm thick chops, trim off white sinew on the sides; loosen meat slightly with a meat beater. Marinate in **1** for one hour.

2 Wash and mince shallot, stir fry in lard until fragant.

3 Heat the wok, add 5C. oil; heat to 180°C (360°F). Dredge pork chop in sweet potato flour and deep fry in oil until golden, drain. Sprinkle on well-mixed **4** and cut to 4 cm long strips.

4 Bring stock to boil, add in **2** and **3** to be the soup.

5 Place noodle in individual bowls, pour over soup; arrange pork chop on top and sprinkle on minced green onion. Serve.

榨菜肉絲湯麵

• *Pickled Mustard and Pork Noodle*

四人份　**serve　4**

榨菜肉絲湯麵 • *Pickled Mustard and Pork Noodle*

熟陽春麵 ----------- 8 8 0 公克
里肌肉 -------------- 3 3 0 公克
榨菜絲、小白菜 各150公克
薑絲 ------------------ 2 0 公克
高湯 ---------------------- 8 杯
蔥段 ---------------------- 5 段
蔥末 ------------------ 2 大匙

1
┌ 水 ---------------- 2 大匙
│ 醬油 ------------- 1 ¼ 大匙
│ 酒、太白粉 ----- 各 1 大匙
└ 味精 ---------------- ¼ 小匙

3
┌ 醬油 ---------------- 1 大匙
│ 鹽 ------------------- 1 小匙
│ 味精 ---------------- ¾ 小匙
└ 胡椒粉、麻油 --- 各 ¼ 小匙

2
┌ 水 ---------------------- ½ 杯
│ 醬油 ------------------ ½ 大匙
│ 鹽、糖、味精、麻油 -----
│ -------------------- 各 ¼ 小匙
└ 胡椒粉 -------------- ⅛ 小匙

1 將里肌肉切絲，入 **1** 料拌勻醃約 1 小時，榨菜絲洗淨瀝乾備用。
2 鍋熱入油 4 大匙燒熱，將肉絲炒熟盛出。鍋中再入油 3 大匙炒香
蔥、薑，再放入榨菜絲及 **2** 料拌炒均勻，最後入肉絲拌勻盛出。
3 麵條置於碗中，高湯加 **3** 料煮開後，入小白菜煮熟淋於麵上，再
上置榨菜肉絲及蔥末即可。
■ 榨菜肉絲刀削湯麵：將熟陽春麵改為熟刀削麵，其餘材料及做法
同榨菜肉絲湯麵。

880g.(2lb.) ----------------------------boiled plain noodle
330g.(11³/₅oz.) -----------------------------------pork fillet
150g.(5⅓oz.)each ------------- shredded pickled mustard
head, baby cabbage
20g.(²/₃oz.) -----------------------------------shredded ginger
8C. --stock
5 sections-- green onion
2T. --minced green onion

1
┌ •2T.water
│ •1¼T.soy sauce
└ •1T.each cooking wine, corn starch

2
┌ •½C.water
│ •½T.soy sauce
│ •¼t.each salt, sugar, sesame oil
└ •⅛t.pepper

3
┌ •1T.soy sauce
│ •1t.salt
└ •¼t.each pepper, sesame oil

1 Shred pork and marinate in **1** for one hour. Rinse
clean pickled mustard head.
2 Heat the wok, add 4T. oil and heat to hot; stir fry pork
until cooked, remove. Add 3T. more oil in the wok,
stir fry green onion and ginger until fragrant; add in
pickled mustard head and **2**, mix evenly. Then stir in
pork, mix thoroughly; remove.
3 Place noodle in individual bowls. Bring stock and **3** to
boil, add in cabbage; boil until cooked. Pour over
noodle, arrange pickled mustard head and pork on
top. Sprinkle on green onion and serve.
■ Pickled Mustard and Pork Shaved Noodle : Replace
boiled plain noodle with boiled shaved noodle. The
rest of materials and methods are the same as above.

雪菜肉絲湯麵 • *Pickled Green and Pork Noodle*

熟陽春麵 ----------- 880公克	高湯 ----------------------- 8杯
雪裡紅 --------------- 500公克	蔥末、紅辣椒末 ------ 各1大匙
里肌肉 --------------- 300公克	

1
- 水 ------------------ 2大匙
- 醬油 --------------- 1¼大匙
- 酒、太白粉 ----- 各1大匙
- 味精 ----------------- ¼小匙

3
- 醬油 ----------------- 4大匙
- 麻油 ----------------- 1小匙
- 胡椒粉 --------------- ¼小匙

2
- 水 ------------------ 2大匙
- 糖、麻油 -------- 各1小匙
- 鹽 -------------------- ½小匙
- 胡椒粉 --------------- ¼小匙

1 里肌肉切絲加 **1** 料醃約30分鐘，炒前拌入油½大匙，雪裡紅洗淨切碎備用。

2 鍋熱入油2大匙燒熱，將肉絲炒熟盛出。鍋中再入油2大匙，入蔥、辣椒爆香，再入雪裡紅略炒，最後入肉絲及 **2** 料炒勻盛出。

3 麵條置於碗中，高湯加 **3** 料煮開後淋於麵上，再上置炒好的雪菜肉絲即可。

880g.(2lb.) ---boiled plain noodle
500g.(17²/₃oz.) ----pickled mustard green

300g.(10½oz.) - pork fillet
8C ---------------------stock
1T.each ----minced green onion, minced red pepper

1
- 2T.water
- 1¼T.soy sauce
- 1T.each cooking wine, corn starch

3
- 4T.soy sauce
- 1t.sesame oil
- ¼t.pepper

2
- 2T.water
- 1t.each sesame oil, sugar
- ½t.salt
- ¼t.pepper

1 Shred pork and marinate in **1** for 30 minutes; mix in ½T.oil before frying. Wash pickled mustard green clean and mince.

2 Heat the wok, add 2T. oil and heat to hot; stir fry pork until cooked, remove. Add 2T. oil to the wok, stir fry green onion and red pepper until fragrant. Add in pickled mustard green, stir fry slightly; stir in pork and **2**, mix evenly. Remove.

3 Place noodle in individual bowls. Bring stock and **3** to boil and pour over the noodle. Arrange pickled mustard green and pork on top, serve.

餛飩麵（雲吞麵）・*Wonton Noodle*

熟陽春麵 ----------- 880公克	高湯 ------------------------ 8 杯		880g.(2lb.) --- boiled plain noodle	32 ------ wonton wrappers
小白菜 ------------- 200公克	榨菜末 ----------------------⅓杯		200g.(7oz.) baby cabbage	8C. --------------------- stock
絞肉 --------------- 150公克	蔥末 --------------------- 5 大匙		150g.(5¼oz.) minced pork	⅓C. ------- minced pickled mustard head
蝦仁 --------------- 100公克	紅蔥頭末 -------------- 2 ½大匙		100g.(3½oz.) ------ shelled shrimp	5T. -- minced green onion
餛飩皮 -------------- 32張				2½T. -- minced red shallot

❶
- 蛋 --------------------⅔個
- 榨菜末、麻油 --各 2 大匙
- 蔥末 ------------------¾大匙
- 鹽、酒、味精 ---各¼小匙
- 糖、胡椒粉 ------各⅛小匙

❷
- 鹽、糖 -------- 各 1 ½小匙
- 烏醋 ------------------ 1 小匙
- 味精 ------------------¼小匙
- 胡椒粉 --------------⅛小匙

1 小白菜洗淨切段，蝦仁去腸泥洗淨剁碎與絞肉、**❶**料攪拌均勻，即為餛飩餡，再以餛飩皮包成餛飩備用。

2 鍋熱入豬油 2 大匙燒熱，入紅蔥頭爆香，再入高湯及 **❷** 料煮開後，入餛飩及小白菜煮熟即為餛飩湯。

3 麵條置於碗中，上灑榨菜末及蔥末，再淋上餛飩湯即可。

❶
- ⅔ egg
- 2T.each minced pickled mustard head, sesame oil
- ¾T. minced green onion
- ¼t.each cooking wine, salt
- ⅛t.each sugar, pepper

❷
- 1½t.each salt, sugar
- 1t.brown vinegar
- ⅛t.pepper

1 Wash cabbage and cut into serving sections. De- vein shrimp and wash clean; chop fine. Mix shrimp with pork and **❶** evenly to be the wonton filling. Wrap filling into wonton wrappers.

2 Heat the wok, add 2T. lard and heat to hot; stir fry shallot until fragrant. Pour in stock and **❷**, bring to boil. Then add in wonton and cabbage, boil until cooked.

3 Place noodle in individual bowls, sprinkle on mustard head and green onion. Pour wonton soup over and served.

切阿麵 · *Chie-Ah Mein*

熟油麵	------------ 800公克		韭菜	------------ 120公克
綠豆芽	------------ 240公克		高湯	------------ 8杯
後腿肉	------------ 180公克		紅蔥頭末	------------ 5大匙

❶
- 鹽 ------------ 1¼小匙
- 味精 ------------ ½小匙
- 胡椒粉 ------------ ⅛小匙

1 豬肉洗淨入高湯中煮熟，取出待涼切5×4公分薄片，韭菜切3公分長段。
2 鍋熱入豬油2½大匙燒熱，入紅蔥頭爆香，再加入高湯及❶料煮開即為麵湯。
3 油麵分四次入竹漏杓內，入滾開水中抖動至麵熱後，扣入碗中，韭菜、綠豆芽亦放入竹漏杓中燙熟置於麵上，最上面再舖以肉片，淋上麵湯即可。

800g.(1¾lb.) -------- boiled yellow noodle
240g.(8²/₅oz.) -------- bean sprout
8C. -------------------- stock

180g.(6⅓oz.) --- pork hind leg
120g.(4¼oz.) -------- chive
5T. ---- minced red shallot

❶
- 1¼t.salt
- ⅛t.pepper

1 Wash pork clean and boil in stock until cooked; lift out and cut into 5 x 4 cm thin slices when cooled. Cut chive into 3 cm sections.
2 Heat the wok, add 2½T. lard and heat to hot; stir fry shallot until fragrant. Add in stock and ❶ , bring to boil.
3 Divide noodle equally into 4 bamboo sieves; lower into boiling water until heated. Lift out and turn into four bowls. Cook chive and bean sprout in the same method, and arrange on top of the noodle; topped with sliced pork. Pour soup over and serve.

擔仔麵 • *Dan-Tze Mein*

熟油麵 -------------- 800公克	高湯 ------------------------- 8杯
絞肉 ----------------- 350公克	紅蔥頭末 --------------------- 1/3杯
綠豆芽 -------------- 240公克	蒜末 --------------------- 1大匙
韭菜 -------------------- 80公克	

1
```
┌ 高湯 ------------------- 1杯
│ 醬油、甜麵醬 各1 1/2大匙
│ 酒 -------------------- 1大匙
│ 糖 -------------------- 1小匙
│ 胡椒粉、味精 --- 各1/2小匙
└ 鹽、五香粉 ------ 各1/4小匙
```

2
```
┌ 鹽、麻油 -------- 各1小匙
│ 味精 ----------------- 1/4小匙
└ 胡椒粉 -------------- 1/8小匙
```

1 鍋熱入油3大匙燒熱，入紅蔥頭、蒜末爆香，續入絞肉炒熟後，再加入 **1** 料拌炒均勻，並以小火燜煮約30分鐘，其間每隔10分鐘翻攪一次，煮好即為肉燥。

2 另鍋中入高湯及 **2** 料煮開，即為麵湯。

3 油麵分四次入竹漏杓內，入滾開水中抖動至麵熱後，扣入碗中，韭菜、綠豆芽以同樣方式燙熟置於麵上，淋上肉燥並加上麵湯即可。

800g.(1 3/4 lb.) -------- boiled yellow noodle	80g.(2 4/5 oz.) ---------- chive
350g.(12 1/3 oz.) ---- minced pork	8C. --------------------- stock
240g.(8 2/5 oz.) bean sprout	1/3 C. ---- minced red shallot
	1T. ---------- minced garlic

1
- 1C.stock
- 1 1/2 T.each soy sauce, sweet soy bean paste
- 1T.cooking wine
- 1t.sugar
- 1/2 t.pepper
- 1/4 t each salt, five spices powder

2
- 1t.each salt, sesame oil
- 1/8 t.pepper

1 Heat the wok, add 3T. oil and heat to hot; stir fry shallot and garlic until fragrant. Add in pork, stir fry until cooked. Then mix in **1** evenly, and simmer for 30 minutes; stir every 10 minutes. This is the meat seasoning sauce.

2 In another pot, bring stock and **2** to boil to be the soup.

3 Divide noodle equally into four bamboo sieves; lower into boiling water until heated. Turn noodle into four bowls. Cook chive and bean sprout in the same method, and arrange on top the noodle. Spoon meat sauce on, and pour soup over. Serve.

白菜肉絲湯麵 • *Chinese Cabbage and Pork Noodle*

熟陽春麵 ------------ 880公克	香菇 ---------------------- 8公克
里肌肉、大白菜 各100公克	高湯 ----------------------- 9杯
綠豆芽、熟筍 ------ 各50公克	蒜末 ---------------------- ½大匙
韭菜 --------------- 10公克	薑末 ---------------------- ⅓大匙

❶
- 鹽 ----------------- 2小匙
- 糖 ----------------- 1小匙
- 味精 ----------------½小匙
- 胡椒粉 --------------⅛小匙

1 里肌肉、大白菜洗淨切絲，綠豆芽洗淨，熟筍切絲，香菇泡軟去蒂切絲，韭菜切段。

2 鍋熱入油2大匙燒熱，炒香蒜末、薑末，再入香菇、大白菜炒香，隨即入高湯煮開，再入里肌肉、筍、麵條及 **❶** 料續煮至入味後，再加韭菜及綠豆芽煮開即可。

■ 喜好芹菜口味者可以添加少許芹菜。

880g.(2lb.) ---boiled plain noodle
100g.(1¾oz.)each ---pork fillet, Chinese cabbage
50g.(3½oz.)each -----bean sprout, boiled bamboo shoot

10g.(⅓oz.) -----------chive
8g.(¼oz.) ------dried black mushroom
9C. --------------------stock
½T. ----------- minced garlic
⅓T. --------minced ginger

❶
- •2t.salt
- •1t.sugar
- •⅛t.pepper

1 Wash clean pork and cabbage, shred both. Wash bean sprout. Shred bamboo. Soften mushroom in warm water and discard stem, shred. Cut chive into serving sections.

2 Heat the wok, add 2T. oil and heat to hot; stir fry garlic and ginger. Add in mushroom and cabbage until soften. Pour in stock and bring to boil. Add in pork, bamboo, noodle and **❶**; cook until noodle tasty. Add in chive and bean sprout, bring to boil and serve.

■ Celery can be added for celery lovers.

家常麵片湯 • *Home Favorite Noodle Pieces*

熟麵片 -------------- ８８０公克	香菇 --------------------- ８公克
小白菜 -------------- ２４０公克	高湯 --------------------- ８杯
里肌肉 -------------- １５０公克	劍蝦 --------------------- ８隻
榨菜 ---------------- １００公克	蔥末 --------------------- ３½大匙
蝦米 ------------------ １５公克	

■ ┌ 麻油 -------------- １大匙
　　├ 鹽 ---------------- １¼小匙
　　├ 味精 ------------- ¼小匙
　　└ 胡椒粉 ---------- ⅛小匙

1 榨菜洗淨與里肌肉均切成３×４公分薄片，劍蝦去腸泥洗淨，香菇泡軟去蒂切片，蝦米泡軟，小白菜洗淨切段備用。

2 鍋熱入油３大匙燒熱，入蝦米及香菇、蔥末爆香後，入肉片拌炒一下，再入高湯及 **■** 料煮開，續入劍蝦、榨菜、小白菜煮熟即為麵湯。

3 麵片置於碗中，淋上麵湯即可。

880g.(2lb.) ---------- boiled noodle pieces	15g.(½oz) ------ dried baby shrimp
240g.(8⅖oz.) --------- baby cabbage	8g.(¼oz.) ------ dried black mushroom
150g.(5⅓oz.) --- pork fillet	8C. -------------------- stock
100g.(3½oz.) ------ pickled mustard head	8 --------------------- shrimp
	3½T. ..minced green onion

■ ┌ •1T.sesame oil
　　├ •1¼t.salt
　　└ •⅛t.pepper

1 Wash clean mustard head and pork, cut both into 3 x 4 cm thin slices. De-vein shrimp and wash clean. Soften mushroom in warm water and discard stem; slice. Soften dried shrimp in warm water. Wash cabbage and cut into serving sections.

2 Heat the wok, add 3T. oil and heat to hot; stir fry dried shrimp, mushroom and green onion until fragrant. Stir in pork and fry slightly. Pour in stock and **■**, bring to boil. Add in shrimp, mustard head, and cabbage; boil until cooked.

3 Place noodle pieces in individual bowls, pour soup over and serve.

家常湯麵 • *Home Favorite Soup Noodle*

熟陽春麵	880公克	香菇	8公克
豬肉	200公克	高湯	8杯
小白菜	160公克	蔥末	5大匙
熟筍	120公克	蛋	2個

❶
- 醬油 ---------------- 2大匙
- 麻油 ---------------- 1小匙
- 鹽、味精 -------- 各¼小匙
- 胡椒粉 -------------- ⅛小匙

1 小白菜洗淨切段，豬肉切4×5公分薄片，香菇泡軟去蒂與筍均切薄片。

2 高湯煮開入豬肉、筍、香菇及❶料煮熟，再將蛋打散入湯汁中，並入小白菜煮熟即為麵湯。

3 麵條置於碗中，將麵湯淋於麵上並灑上蔥末即可。

880g.(2lb.) ---boiled plain noodle
200g.(7oz.) ----------pork
160g.(5³/₅oz.) --------baby cabbage
120g.(4¼oz.) ------boiled bamboo shoot

8g.(¼oz.) ------dried black mushroom
8C. --------------------stock
5T. --minced green onion
2 -----------------------eggs

❶
- •2T.soy sauce
- •1t.sesame oil
- •¼t.salt
- •⅛t.pepper

1 Wash cabbage and cut into serving sections. Cut pork into 4 x 5 cm thin slices. Soften mushroom in warm water and discard stem; slice thin. Slice bamboo thin.

2 Bring stock to boil, add in pork, bamboo, mushroom and ❶ ; boil until all cooked. Pour in beatened eggs, and cabbage; boiled until cabbage cooked.

3 Place noodle in individual bowls, pour soup over; sprinkle on green onion and serve.

叉燒湯麵 • *Bar-B-Q Pork Noodle*

熟陽春麵 ----------- ８８０公克	高湯 ------------------------- ８杯
梅花肉、芥藍菜 各３００公克	蔥段 ------------------------- ５段
薑絲 -------------------- ２０公克	

❶
```
┌ 水 -------------------- ¼杯
│ 糖 -------------------- ５大匙
│ 醬油、酒、鹽 --各１大匙
│ 蔥末 ----------------- ¾大匙
│ 海山醬 -------------- ½大匙
└ 食用紅色６號 ------- 少許
```

❷
```
┌ 醬油 ----------------- ３大匙
│ 蠔油 ----------------- １大匙
│ 麻油 ----------------- １½小匙
│ 酒、胡椒粉 ------ 各¾小匙
└ 糖、味精 --------- 各½小匙
```

1 梅花肉切長條，以 **❶** 料醃約１２小時，烤箱上、下火調至２５０
　℃預熱後，將肉置於烤架上入烤箱烘烤，並時時刷上醃肉汁，烤
　至肉熟透取出，待涼切薄片。

2 鍋熱入油３大匙燒熱，入蔥、薑炒香，續入高湯煮開，再入芥藍
　菜煮熟並加 **❷** 料煮開即為麵湯。

3 麵條置於碗中，淋上麵湯，再放入叉燒肉片即可。

880g.(2lb.) --- boiled plain noodle
300g.(10½oz.)each -- pork shoulder, gailan
20g.(²⁄₃oz.) ------ shredded ginger
8C. --------------------- stock
5 sections ---- green onion

❶
```
• ¼C.water
• 5T.sugar
• 1T .each  soy sauce,
  cooking wine, salt
• ¾T.minced garlic
• ½T.Ho-sien sauce
• dash  red food
  coloring
```

❷
```
• 3T.soy sauce
• 1T.oyster sauce
• 1½t.sesame oil
• ¾t.each  cooking
  wine, pepper
• ½t. sugar
```

1 Cut pork into large long strips marinate in **❶** for 12 hours. Pre-heat oven to 250°C (482°F), bake pork on a rack; baste with marinate often, bake until pork thoroughly cooked. Slice thin when cooled.

2 Heat the wok, add 3T. oil and heat to hot; stir fry green onion and ginger until fragrant. Add in stock and bring to boil. Then add in gailan, cook until done. Mix in **❷** and boil again.

3 Place noodle in individual bowls, pour soup over; arrange pork slices on top and serve.

41

香腸拉麵 • *Sausage Noodle*

熟拉麵 ------------- ８８０公克	高湯 ----------------------- ８杯	880g.(2lb.) --- boild hand-pulled noodle	8C. --------------------- stock
香腸 ---------------- ３５０公克	蔥末、紅蔥頭末 ------ 各４大匙	350g.(12⅓oz.) --- Chinese sausage	4T.each ---- minced green onion, minced shallot
青江菜 ------------- ３００公克	薑片 ------------------------ ２片	300g.(10½oz.) -- bok choy	2 slices -------------- ginger

1 ［
酒 -------------------- １大匙
鹽 -------------------- １¼小匙
味精、糖 --------- 各½小匙
胡椒粉 -------------- ⅓小匙
］

1 ［
• 1T.cooking wine
• 1¼t.salt
• ½t.sugar
• ⅓t.pepper
］

1 鍋熱入油３大匙燒熱，將香腸煎至表面酥脆撈起，待涼切成斜片，青江菜一葉葉剝開洗淨備用。

2 鍋再熱入油１大匙燒熱，入薑片、紅蔥頭爆香，續入 **1** 料及高湯煮開，再入青江菜煮開即為麵湯。

3 拉麵置於碗中，上置香腸，再灑上蔥末並淋上麵湯即可。

1 Heat the wok, add 3T. oil and heat to hot; saute sausage until surface crispy, cut into slanting slices when cooled. Split bok choy, leave by leave, and wash clean.

2 Add 1T. oil in wok and heat to hot; stir fry ginger and shallot until fragrant. Add in **1** and stock, bring to boil, add in bok choy and boil again.

3 Place noodle in individual bowls, arrange sausage slices on top; sprinkle on green onion. Pour soup over noodle and serve.

當歸鴨麵線 • *Duck and Chinese Herbs Soup Noodle*

熟黑麵線 ---------- 760公克　　鹽 ----------------- 1小匙
鴨肉 -------------- 700公克

1　┌ 黑棗 ------------- 80公克
　　│ 當歸、枸杞 -- 各40公克
　　│ 川芎、熟地 -- 各16公克
　　│ 酒 ----------------- 1½杯
　　│ 蔥段 ------------- 15段
　　└ 老薑片 ----------- 4片

1　鴨肉洗淨，剁成3×5公分塊狀，入沸水中川燙，取出洗淨備用。

2　將鴨肉、水9杯及**1**料入鍋煮開改小火續煮約1½小時後，再加鹽調味即為當歸鴨湯。

3　麵線置於碗中，淋上當歸鴨湯即可。

760g.(1²/₃lb.) -------- boiled　　700g.(1½lb.) ---------- duck
black noodle string　　　　　　　1t. ---------------------- salt

1　┌ •80g.(2⁴/₅oz.) black prune
　　│ •40g.(1²/₅oz.)each Chinese angelica root, medlar
　　│ •16g.(³/₅oz.) each cuidium officinale, Rehmannia
　　│ praeparatum
　　│ •1½C.cooking wine
　　│ •15 sections green onion
　　└ •4 slices aged ginger

1 Wash clean duck meat, cut into 3 x 5 cm serving pieces. Scald in boiling water and rinse clean.

2 Put duck, 9C. water, and **1** in a pot and bring to boil; simmer over low heat for one and half hour. Season with salt.

3 Place noodle string in individual bowls, pour over soup and serve.

麻油雞麵線 • *Sesame Oil Chicken Noodle String*

熟白麵線	880公克	米酒	2½杯
雞半隻	750公克	黑麻油	5大匙
老薑片	80公克		

1 ┌ 冰糖 -------------- ½大匙
　　└ 鹽 -------------- 1小匙

1 雞洗淨剁成2．5×5公分塊狀，鍋熱入黑麻油燒熱，入薑片爆香後，續入雞塊拌炒至淡褐色，再加酒煮開，隨即加 **1** 料及水7杯煮開改小火煮50分鐘，即為麻油雞湯。

2 麵線置於碗中，淋上麻油雞湯即可。

880g.(2lb.) --boiled white noodle string	80g.(2⁴/₅oz.) --------sliced aged ginger
750g.(1³/₅lb.) half chicken	2½C. -------cooking wine
	5T. ------black sesame oil

1 ┌ •½T.crystal sugar
　　└ •1t.salt

1 Wash chicken clean and cut into 2.5 x 5 cm serving pieces. Heat the wok, add in sesame oil; stir fry ginger until fragrant. Then add in chicken, stir fry until light brown; pour in wine and bring to boil. Mix in **1** and 7C. water, simmer over low heat for 50 minutes.

2 Place noodle string in individual bowls, pour over soup and serve.

四人份　**serve 4**

豬腳麵線 • *Pig Hoof Noodle String*

熟白麵線	880公克	蔥段	8段
豬腳	600公克	薑片	8片

1 ┌ 酒 -------------- 1大匙　　**2** ┌ 薑絲 -------------- 20公克
　　└ 鹽 -------------- 2小匙　　　　└ 味精 --------------½小匙

1 豬腳去毛，剁成8塊，入開水川燙，撈起洗淨，蔥段、薑片及**1**料加水16杯煮開，入豬腳再煮開，改小火燜煮1小時至肉熟爛，肉取出，湯汁瀝去蔥、薑，另加 **2** 料煮開即為豬腳湯。

2 麵線置於碗中，舖上豬腳再淋上豬腳湯拌勻即可。

880g.(2lb.) --boiled white noodle string	8 sections ----green onion
600g.(1⅓lb.) -----pig hoof	8 slices ---------------ginger

1 ┌ •1T.cooking wine　　**2** ┌ •20g.(²/₃oz.) shredded
　　└ •2t.salt　　　　　　　　└ ginger

1 Pluck pig hoof and chop into 8 serving pieces; scald in boiling water, lift out and rinse clean. Add 16C. water with green onion, ginger and **1** together and bring to boil. Add in pig hoof and bring to boil again, then simmer over low heat for one hour until tender. Remove pig hoof from the soup, discard green onion and ginger, add in **2** and boil again to be noodle soup.

2 Place noodle in individual bowls, arrange pig hoof on top; pour soup over and serve.

　四人份　**serve 4**

豬肝湯麵 • *Pork Liver Soup Noodle*

熟陽春麵	880公克	高湯	8杯
豬肝	300公克	蔥段	5段
菠菜、洋蔥絲	各200公克		

❶
- 太白粉 -------------- 1 大匙
- 味精 ------------------ ½ 小匙
- 鹽 -------------------- ¼ 小匙

❷
- 烏醋、麻油 ------ 各2 小匙
- 醬油、酒、鹽 ---各¾ 小匙
- 胡椒粉、味精 --- 各½ 小匙

1 豬肝切薄片，以 ❶ 料醃約1小時，菠菜洗淨切段備用。
2 鍋熱入油3杯燒至六分熱（140℃），入豬肝過油至熟撈起。
3 鍋內留油3大匙燒熱，入蔥段、洋蔥絲炒香，隨即入高湯煮開，再入菠菜及 ❷ 料煮開，淋於麵上，上置豬肝即可。

880g.(2lb.) --- boiled plain noodle
300g.(10½oz.) -- pork liver

200g.(7oz.)each - spinach, shredded onion
8C. --------------------- stock
5 sections ---- green onion

❶
- 1T.corn starch
- ¼t.salt

❷
- 2t.each brown vinegar, sesame oil
- ¾t.each soy sauce, cooking wine, salt
- ½t.pepper

1 Slice pork liver thin, marinate with ❶ for one hour. Clean spinach and cut into serving sections.
2 Heat the wok, add 3C. oil and heat to 140℃ (284°F); soak liver in hot oil until cooked.
3 Keep 3T. oil in the wok and heat hot; stir fry green onion and onion until fragrant. Add in stock and bring to boil, add in spinach and ❷; bring to boil again. Pour soup over noodle and arrange liver on top. Serve hot.

四人份　serve 4

開陽白菜麵 • *Chinese Cabbage and Dried Shrimp Noodle*

熟陽春麵	880公克	高湯	8杯
大白菜絲	460公克		

❶
- 洋蔥丁 -------- 200公克
- 蝦米 -------------- 40公克
- 蔥末 ----------------- 5大匙

❷
- 醬油、鹽、麻油各1 小匙
- 味精、酒 --------- 各½ 小匙
- 胡椒粉 ---------------- ⅛ 小匙

1 蝦米泡軟，鍋熱入油3大匙燒熱，入 ❶ 料爆香，續入大白菜絲炒軟，再入高湯及 ❷ 料煮開即為麵湯。
2 麵條置於碗中，再淋上麵湯即可。

880g.(2lb.) --- boiled plain noodle

460g.(1lb.) ------ shredded Chinese cabbage
8C. --------------------- stock

❶
- 200g.(7oz.) diced onion
- 40g.(1²/₄oz.) dried baby shrimp
- 5T.minced green onion

❷
- 1t.each soy sauce, salt, sesame oil
- ½t.cooking wine
- ⅛t.pepper

1 Soak shrimp in water to soften, shred cabbage. Heat the wok, add 3T. oil and heat to hot; stir fry ❶ until fragrant. Stir in cabbage, fry until soften; add in stock and ❷, bring to boil to be noodle soup.
2 Place noodle in individual bowls, pour over soup and serve.

四人份　serve 4

雞腿湯麵

• *Noodle with Chicken Leg*

四人份　**serve　4**

雞腿湯麵 · *Noodle with Chicken Leg*

雞腿四隻 -----------	9 0 0 公克
熟陽春麵 -----------	8 8 0 公克
雪裡紅 --------------	1 5 0 公克
高湯 ------------------	8 杯
蛋黃 ------------------	2 個
太白粉 ------------------	5 大匙

1
- 太白粉、醬油 --各 2 大匙
- 糖、酒 ------------ 各½大匙
- 五香粉、胡椒粉 各⅓小匙

2
- 水 ---------------------- ¼杯
- 醬油 ------------------ ½大匙
- 鹽、味精、糖、酒 --------
  ------------------------- 各¼小匙
- 胡椒粉、麻油 --- 各⅛小匙

3
- 蔥末 -------------- 2½大匙
- 醬油 ----------------- 2 小匙
- 麻油 ----------------- 1 小匙
- 鹽、味精、胡椒粉 --------
  --------------------- 各½小匙

1 雞腿洗淨，在肉厚處劃開，加 **1** 料拌醃約 1 小時，炸前再加入蛋黃並沾上太白粉。

2 雪裡紅洗淨切碎，鍋熱入油 2 大匙燒熱，入雪裡紅拌炒，再入**2**料炒勻盛出。

3 鍋熱入油 5 杯燒至八分熱（1 8 0℃），入雞腿炸至表面呈金黃色撈出。

4 麵條置於碗中，高湯加 **3** 料煮開淋於麵上，上置雪裡紅、雞腿即可。

900g.(2lb.) ---------------------------	4 pieces chicken legs
880g.(2lb.) ---------------------------	boiled plain noodle
150g.(5⅓oz.)--------------------------	pickled mustard green
8C. --------------------------------------	stock
2 ---	egg yolk
5T. --------------------------------------	corn starch

1
- 2T.each corn starch, soy sauce
- ½T.each sugar, cooking wine
- ⅓t.each five spices powder, pepper

2
- ¼C.water
- ½T.soy sauce
- ¼t.each salt, sugar, cooking wine
- ⅛t.each pepper, sesame oil

3
- 2½T.minced green onion
- 2t.soy sauce
- 1t.sesame oil
- ½t.each salt, pepper

1 Clean chicken leg, cut slits at thickest part; marinate with **1** for one hour. Before frying, add in egg yolk and dredge in corn starch.

2 Wash pickled mustard green and chop. Heat the wok, add 2T. oil and heat hot; stir fry pickled mustard green, mix in **2** evenly.

3 Heat the wok, add 5C. oil and heat to 180℃ (356°F). Deep fry chicken leg until golden.

4 Place noodle in individual bowls. Bring stock to boil with **3**, and pour over noodle. Arrange pickled mustard green and chicken leg on top and serve.

•Soup Noodle with Assorted Meats and Seafood

四人份　serve　4

什錦湯麵 • *Soup Noodle with Assorted Meats and Seafood*

熟陽春麵 ------------ ８８０公克
發泡魷魚 ------------ ３００公克
熟筍 ----------------- １２０公克
雞胸肉、鴨肫、豬肝 -----------
--------------------- 各９０公克
豌豆莢 --------------- ８０公克
胡蘿蔔 --------------- ６０公克
薑絲 ----------------- １０公克
香菇 ------------------- ４公克
高湯 ------------------- ８杯
鮮蝦 １２隻（約１４０公克）
熟鵪鶉蛋 ------------- １２個
蔥段 ------------------- ５段

1 ┌ 太白粉 -------------- ½小匙
　　└ 鹽 ------------------- ⅛小匙

2 ┌ 太白粉 ------------- 1小匙
　　└ 鹽 ------------------- ¼小匙

3 ┌ 醬油 ---------------- ２大匙
　　│ 酒 ------------------- １大匙
　　│ 鹽、麻油 -------- 各１小匙
　　│ 味精 ---------------- ½小匙
　　└ 胡椒粉 ------------- ⅛小匙

1 鮮蝦洗淨去腸泥，魷魚切成５×２公分條狀，雞胸肉切４×５公分薄片，入 **1** 料醃約３０分鐘，豬肝切４×５公分薄片，與切花刀的鴨肫同以 **2** 料醃３０分鐘備用。

2 筍及胡蘿蔔切成３×４公分薄片，入鍋川燙，碗豆莢去老纖維洗淨，香菇泡軟去蒂。

3 鍋熱入油４大匙，入薑絲、雞肉、豬肝、魷魚、鴨肫、筍及胡蘿蔔略炒，續入高湯煮開後，再入鮮蝦、鵪鶉蛋、豌豆莢、香菇及蔥段與 **3** 料煮熟，淋於麵條上即可。

880g. (2lb.) ---------------------------- boiled plain noodle
300g. (10½oz.) ---------------------------- soaked squid
120g. (4¼oz.) ------------------------ boiled bamboo shoot
90g. (3⅕oz.) each -------- chicken breast, pork liver, duck giblet
80g.(2⅘oz.) ---------------------------------- snow pea pod
60g.(2⅑oz.) --------------------------------------- carrot
10g.(⅓oz.) ------------------------------ shredded ginger
4g.(⅐oz.) ------------------------- dried black mushroom
8C. --- stock
12 --------------------- boiled and shelled quail eggs
12(140g./5oz.) ------------------------------- shrimp
5 sections ----------------------------- green onion

1 ┌ • ½t.corn starch
　　└ • ⅛t.salt

2 ┌ • 1t.corn starch
　　└ • ¼t.salt

3 ┌ • 2T.soy sauce
　　│ • 1T.cooking wine
　　│ • 1t.each salt, sesame oil
　　└ • ⅛t.pepper

1 Clean and devein shrimp; cut squid into 5x2 cm strips. Slice chicken breast into 4x5 cm thin slices; marinate with **1** for 30 minutes. Slice pork liver into 4x5 cm thin slices, cut duck giblet into serving pieces with diagonal cuts on the surface; marinate both with **2** for 30 minutes.

2 Cut bamboo and carrot into 3x4 thin slices; parboil. Discard tough fibers of pea pod and wash clean. Soften mushroom with warm water and discard stems.

3 Heat the wok, add 4T. oil. Stir fry ginger, chicken, liver, squid, giblet, bamboo, and carrot. Add in stock and bring to boil; then add in shrimp, eggs, pea pod, mushroom, green onion, and **3** , boil until all ingredients are cooked. Pour over noodle and serve hot.

翡翠酸辣湯麵 • *Sour Spicy Spinach Noodle*

熟菠菜麵	880公克	高湯	8杯
雞胸肉	240公克	榨菜末	1⅓杯
小白菜	160公克	蔥末	5大匙
蝦米	30公克		

1〔 鹽 -------- ¼小匙
　　胡椒粉 ---- ⅛小匙

3〔 鎮江醋 -------- ¾杯
　　醬油、辣油 -- 各5大匙
　　味精 -------- ½小匙

2〔 麻油 ------ 1小匙
　　味精 ------ ⅛小匙

1 雞胸肉洗淨以 **1** 料醃約30分鐘，入鍋大火蒸8分鐘，取出待涼剝絲備用。
2 蝦米洗淨切末以 **2** 料拌醃，入鍋大火蒸4分鐘，小白菜洗淨切段燙熟。
3 麵條置於碗中，上置榨菜末、雞絲、蝦米、蔥末、小白菜及**3**料，再淋上煮開的高湯拌勻即可。
■ 酸辣湯麵：將熟菠菜麵改為熟陽春麵，其餘材料及做法同翡翠酸辣湯麵。

880g.(2lb.)	boiled spinach noodle	30g.(1oz.)	dried baby shrimp
240g.(8²/₅oz.)	chicken breast	8C.	stock
160g.(5³/₅oz.)	baby cabbage	1⅓C.	minced pickled mustard head
		5T.	minced green onion

1〔 • ¼t.salt
　　• ⅛t.pepper

3〔 • ¾C.brown vinegar
　　• 5T.each soy sauce, chili oil

2 • 1t.sesame oil

1 Wash chicken breast clean and marinate with **1** for 30 minutes; steam over high heat for 8 minutes. When cooled, shred by hand.
2 Wash shrimp and chop fine, marinate with **2** ; steam over high heat for 4 minutes. Boil cabbage until cooked.
3 Place noodle in individual bowls, arrange pickled mustard head, chicken, shrimp, green onion, cabbage, and **3** on top. Pour hot stock over, mix well and serve.
■ Sour Spicy Noodle : Replace boild spinach noodle with boild plain noodle. The rest of materials and methods are the same as above.

月見麵 • *Egg and Taro Noodle*

熟陽春麵 ------------ 8 8 0 公克	高湯 ------------------------ 9 杯	880g.(2lb.) --- boiled plain noodle	9C. ---------------------stock
芋頭 ----------------- 6 0 0 公克	蛋 -------------------------- 4 個	600g.(1⅓lb.) ---------- taro	4 ----------------------- eggs
豆苗嬰 -------------- 1 0 0 公克	紫菜海苔粉 ------------ 1 ⅓ 大匙	100g.(3½oz.) - pea pod tip	1⅓T. -- seasoned seaweed powder
柴魚片 -------------------- 8 公克		8g.(¼oz.) - dried fish flake	

1
- 醬油 ----------------- 3 大匙
- 味醂、酒 -----各 2 大匙
- 糖、麻油 ------ 各 1 ½ 大匙
- 蠔油 ---------------- 2 小匙
- 鹽 ----------------- 1 ½ 小匙
- 味精 ----------------- ¾ 小匙
- 胡椒粉 ------------- ¼ 小匙

1
- •3T.soy sauce
- •2T. each mirin, cooking wine
- •1½T. each sugar, sesame oil
- •2t.oyster sauce
- •1½t.salt
- •¼t.pepper

1 芋頭去皮切 0．8 × 5 公分條狀，鍋熱入油 3 杯燒至八分熱（約 1 8 0 ℃），入芋頭炸熟瀝乾，豆苗嬰洗淨備用。

2 鍋熱入高湯、柴魚片、**1**料及芋頭煮開後，續入麵條再煮開，放入豆苗嬰及蛋煮至蛋白熟蛋黃未熟，再灑上紫菜海苔粉即可。

1 Peel taro and cut into 0.8 x 5 cm strips. Heat the wok, add 3C. oil and heat to 180°C (356°F), deep fry taro until cooked; remove and drain. Wash clean pea pod tips.

2 Heat the wok, add in stock, fish flake, **1**, and taro; bring to boil and add in noodle, bring to boil again. Add in pea pod tips and eggs until egg white cooked, egg yolk should still be soft. Sprinkle on seaweed powder and serve.

四人份　**serve 4**

海鮮炒麵 • *Seafood Fried Noodle*

兩面黃 ------------- 680公克		豆瓣醬 ------------------- 1 小匙	

1
油菜 ---------- 200公克
花枝、蝦仁、海參、熟草
菇 ---------- 各120公克
熟筍 ---------- 100公克
胡蘿蔔 ---------- 60公克

2
酒、太白粉 ----- 各2小匙
鹽、胡椒粉 ------ 各¼小匙

3
高湯 -------------------- 2 杯
醬油 ------------------ 2 大匙
太白粉 ------------ 1⅓大匙
酒 -------------------- 2 小匙
鹽 -------------------- ½小匙
味精、胡椒粉 --- 各¼小匙

1 蝦仁去腸泥洗淨，花枝、海參亦洗淨切片，三者以 **2** 料拌醃，草菇、熟筍、胡蘿蔔均切片，油菜洗淨切 3 公分長段。
2 鍋熱入油 3 大匙燒熱，入豆瓣醬炒香，再入 **1** 料炒拌均勻，續入 **3** 料煮開，淋於兩面黃上即可。

680g.(1½lb.) ------- noodle pancake   1t. --------soy bean paste

1
• 200g.(7oz.) rape
• 120g.(4¼oz.) each squid, shelled shrimp, sea cucumber, boiled straw mushroom
• 100g.(3½oz.) canned or boiled bamboo shoot
• 60g.(2⅑oz.) carrot

2
• 2t.each cooking wine, corn starch
• ¼t.each salt, pepper

3
• 2C.stock
• 2T.soy sauce
• 1⅓T.corn starch
• 2t.cooking wine
• ½t.salt
• ¼t.pepper

1 De-vein shrimp and wash clean. Wash clean squid and sea cucumber, slice. Marinate all three in **2** . Slice mushroom, bamboo, and carrot. Wash rape clean and cut into 3 cm sections.
2 Heat the wok, add 3T. oil and heat to hot; stir fry soy bean paste until fragrant. Stir in **1** to fry, mix evenly. Add in **3** and bring to boil. Pour over noodle pancake and serve.

蝦仁炒麵 • *Shrimp Fried Noodle*

炸麵 ---------------- 3 6 0 公克　　　　小白菜 -------------- 2 4 0 公克

1
- 蝦仁 ---------- 1 6 0 公克
- 熟筍 ---------- 1 2 0 公克
- 濕木耳 ---------- 6 0 公克
- 豌豆莢 ---------- 5 0 公克

2
- 蛋白 ------------------ ½個
- 太白粉 ---------- 1 ⅓大匙
- 酒 -------------- 2 小匙
- 鹽、胡椒粉 ------ 各¼小匙

3
- 高湯 -------------------- 3 杯
- 酒 -------------------- 2 小匙
- 鹽 -------------------- 1 小匙
- 味精 ------------------ ½小匙
- 胡椒粉 --------------- ¼小匙

4
- 水 -------------- 4 大匙
- 太白粉 ---------- 2 大匙

1 蝦仁去腸泥洗淨，入 **2** 料拌醃，木耳去蒂與熟筍均切片，豌豆莢去老纖維洗淨，小白菜洗淨切 3 公分長段。

2 鍋熱入油 4 大匙燒熱，依次入蝦仁、熟筍、木耳、豌豆莢炒熟盛起備用。

3 **3** 料煮開，入 **1** 料及小白菜再煮開，以 **4** 料芶芡，淋於炸麵上即可。

■ 蝦仁炒麵之炸麵可以伊麵取代。

360g.(12²/₃oz.) ------- deep fried noodle

240g.(8²/₅oz.) --------- baby cabbage

1
- •160g.(5³/₅oz.) shelled shrimp
- •120g.(4¼oz.) canned or boiled bamboo shoot
- •60g.(2oz.) soaked black wood ear
- •50g.(1³/₄oz.) pea pod

2
- •½ egg white
- •1⅓T.corn starch
- •2t.cooking wine
- •¼t.each salt, pepper

3
- •3C.stock
- •2t.cooking wine
- •1t.salt
- •¼t.pepper

4
- •4T.water
- •2T.corn starch

1 De-vein shrimp and wash clean, marinate in **2** . Discard stem of wood ear; cut, also bamboo, into slices. Discard tough fibers of pea pod and wash clean. Wash cabbage and cut into 3 cm sections.

2 Heat the wok, add 4T. oil and heat to hot; stir fry by order of shrimp, bamboo, wood ear, and pea pod together. Remove.

3 Bring **3** to boil, add in **1** and cabbage to boil again. Thicken with **4** , pour over deep fried noodle and serve.

■ Deep fried noodle can be replaced by e-fu noodle.

青椒牛肉麵 • *Beef and Green Pepper Fried Noodle*

熟陽春麵 ---------- 880公克	熟筍 ----------------- 160公克
牛肉、青椒 ------ 各240公克	蔥段 ---------------------- 20段

1
蛋 ------------------------ 1個	
油 ----------------------- 2大匙	
醬油 --------------------- 1大匙	
太白粉、酒 ----- 各2小匙	

2
高湯 -------------------- ½杯
醬油 ----------------- 2大匙
酒 -------------------- 2小匙
糖、麻油 -------- 各1小匙
鹽 ---------------------- ½小匙
味精、胡椒粉 --- 各¼小匙

1 牛肉切薄片，入 **1** 料拌醃，青椒去籽洗淨與筍同切1．5公分寬之長形。

2 鍋熱入油4杯燒至五分熱（120℃），入牛肉過油，至變色撈起瀝油，再入青椒過油，隨即撈起瀝油備用。

3 鍋內留油2大匙，入蔥段爆香，續入牛肉、青椒、筍、麵條及 **2** 料炒拌均勻即可。

■ **青椒牛肉刀削麵**：將熟陽春麵改為熟刀削麵，其餘材料及做法同青椒牛肉麵。

880g.(2lb.) --- boiled plain noodle
240g.(8²/₅oz.)each -- beef, green pepper

160g.(5³/₅oz.) -- canned or boiled bamboo shoot
20 sections -- green onion

1
- •1 egg
- •2T.oil
- •1T.soy sauce
- •2t.each corn starch, cooking wine

2
- •½C.stock
- •2T.soy sauce
- •2t.cooking wine
- •1t.each sugar, sesame oil
- •½t.salt
- •¼t.pepper

1 Shred beef thin, marinate in **1** . Discard seeds in green pepper and cut, also bamboo, into 1.5 cm long strips.

2 Heat the wok, add 4C. oil and heat to 120°C (248°F); soak beef in hot oil until color pales, lift out. Soak green pepper slightly and lift out.

3 Keep 2T. oil in the wok, stir fry green onion until fragrant. Stir in beef, green pepper, bamboo, noodle, and **2** ; Mix and heat well. Serve.

■ Beef and Green Pepper Fried Shaved Noodle : Replace boiled plain noodle with boiled shaved noodle. The rest of materials and methods are the same as above.

酸菜牛肉炒麵 • *Beef and Sour Mustard Fried Noodle*

兩面黃 -------------- ６８０公克	酸菜梗、熟筍 --- 各１６０公克	
牛肉 ----------------- ２００公克	蔥末 --------------------- ２½大匙	

❶
- 蛋 ----------------------- 1個
- 油 ----------------------- 2大匙
- 醬油 ------------------- 1大匙
- 太白粉 ------------- 2小匙
- 酒 --------------------- 1小匙
- 胡椒粉、小蘇打 各¼小匙

❷
- 高湯 -------------------- 2杯
- 醬油 ----------------- 2大匙
- 太白粉 ------------- 1大匙
- 酒 --------------------- 2小匙
- 麻油 ----------------- 1小匙
- 鹽、味精 -------- 各¼小匙

1 牛肉逆紋切絲狀，入 ❶ 料拌醃，酸菜切絲狀，浸泡清水中１０至２０分鐘以降低鹹味，筍切與酸菜大小同。

2 鍋熱入油４杯燒至五分熱（１２０℃），入牛肉過油至變色，隨即撈起瀝油。

3 鍋內留油２大匙燒熱，爆香蔥末，續入酸菜絲、筍絲、牛肉絲炒勻，再入 ❷ 料煮開，淋於兩面黃上即可。

680g.(1½lb.) ------- noodle pancake
200g.(7oz.) ------------ beef

160g.(5³⁄₅oz.)each --- sour mustard stem, canned or boiled bamboo shoot
2½T.- minced green onion

❶
- 1 egg
- 2T.oil
- 1T.soy sauce
- 2t.corn starch
- 1t.cooking wine
- ¼t.each pepper, baking soda

❷
- 2C.stock
- 2T.soy sauce
- 1T.corn starch
- 2t.cooking wine
- 1t.sesame oil
- ¼t.salt

1 Shred beef against the grain, marinate in ❶. Cut sour mustard into shreds, soak in water for 10 to 20 minutes to reduce saltiness. Shred bamboo as sour mustard.

2 Heat the wok, add 4C. oil and heat to 120°C (248°F); soak beef in hot oil until beef turns slightly pale, remove and drain.

3 Keep 2T. oil in the wok and heat to hot, stir fry green onion. Add in sour mustard, bamboo, and beef; mix evenly. Pour in ❷ and bring to boil. Pour over noodle pancake and serve

四人份　**serve 4**

牛肉炸麵 • *Beef Over Deep Fried Noodle*

炸麵 ------------------ ３６０公克	熟筍、熟洋菇 --- 各１００公克
大白菜 ------------- ２４０公克	豌豆莢 ------------------ ７０公克
牛肉 ------------- ２００公克	

1
- 蛋 ------------------ 1個
- 酒 ------------------ 1⅓大匙
- 太白粉、油 ----- 各1大匙
- 醬油 --------------- 1小匙
- 鹽 --------------- ½小匙
- 胡椒粉 ------------- ¼小匙

2
- 高湯 ------------------ 3杯
- 醬油 ------------------ 2大匙
- 太白粉 ------------ 1⅓大匙
- 鹽 --------------------- ½小匙
- 胡椒粉 -------------- ¼小匙

1 牛肉切４×１公分薄條，入 **1** 料拌醃，大白菜、熟筍切成豌豆莢大小的片狀，豌豆莢去老纖維洗淨，洋菇切薄片。

2 鍋熱入油４杯燒至五分熱（１２０℃），入牛肉過油至變色即撈起瀝油，再入其他蔬菜過油，隨即撈起瀝油備用。

3 **2** 料入鍋煮開，續入 **2** 項之材料煮開，再淋於炸麵上即可。

■ 牛肉伊麵：將炸麵改為伊麵，其餘材料及做法同牛肉炸麵。

360g.(12²/₃oz.) ------- deep fried noodle
240g.(8²/₅oz.) ----- Chinese cabbage

200g.(7oz.) ----------- beef
100g.(3½oz.) each ------- boiled mushroom, boiled bamboo shoot
70g.(2½oz.) ------ pea pod

1
- 1 egg
- 1⅓T.cooking wine
- 1T.each corn starch, oil
- 1t.soy sauce
- ½t.salt
- ¼t.pepper

2
- 3C.stock
- 2T.soy sauce
- 1⅓T.corn starch
- ½t.salt
- ¼t.pepper

1 Cut beef into 4 x 1 cm thin stirps, marinate in **1** . Cut cabbage and bamboo into same size as pea pod. Discard tough fiber of pea pod and wash clean. Slice mushroom.

2 Heat the wok, add 4C. oil and heat to 120℃ (248°F); soak beef in hot oil until color pales, lift out and drian. Then soak other vegetables in hot oil, lift out and drain.

3 Bring **2** to boil, add in all materials in **2** to boil. Pour over deep fried noodle and serve.

■ Beef Over E-Fu Noodle : Replace deep fried noodle with e-fu noodle.The rest of materials and methods are the same as above.

沙茶牛肉炒麵 •*Sha-Cha Beef Fried Noodle*

熟油麵 -------------- ８００公克
空心菜（或芥藍菜）------------
---------------------- ４００公克

牛肉 ------------------ ２００公克

1⎡ 蔥末、沙茶醬 --各２大匙
⎣ 薑末、蒜末 -----各２小匙

2⎡ 水 ------------------- ３大匙
⎢ 太白粉 ------------ １大匙
⎢ 油、醬油 -------- 各２小匙
⎢ 酒 ------------------ １小匙
⎣ 糖 ------------------½小匙

3⎡ 高湯 -------------------- １杯
⎢ 醬油 ------------------- ２大匙
⎢ 鹽、味精 --------- 各½小匙
⎣ 胡椒粉 -------------- ¼小匙

1 牛肉切片，入 **2** 料拌醃，空心菜去老硬部分，洗淨切３公分長段。

2 鍋熱入油２大匙燒熱，入牛肉炒至變色，再入空心菜略炒盛出。

3 鍋再熱入油２大匙燒熱，入 **1** 料爆香，再依次入油麵、**3** 料及牛肉絲炒拌均勻即可。

800g.(1½lb.) -------- boiled yellow noodle
200g.(7oz.) ------------ beef

400g.(14oz.) -------- water convolvulus

1⎡ •2T.each minced green onion, sha-cha paste
⎣ •2t.each minced ginger, minced garlic

2⎡ •3T.water
⎢ •1T.corn starch
⎢ •2t.each oil, soy sauce
⎢ •1t.cooking wine
⎣ •½t.sugar

3⎡ •1C.stock
⎢ •2T.soy sauce
⎢ •½t.salt
⎣ •¼t.pepper

1 Shred beef thin, and marinate in **2** . Discard tough fiber of water convolvulus, wash clean and cut into 3 cm sections.

2 Heat the wok, add 2T. oil and heat to hot; stir fry beef until color pales. Add in vegetable to fry slightly. Remove.

3 Heat the wok again, add 2T. oil and heat to hot; stir fry **1** until fragrant. Add in by order of noodle, **3** , and beef; stir fry evenly and heat well. Serve.

四人份　serve 4

辣味炒麵 · *Spicy Fried Noodle*

熟陽春麵 ------------ ８８０公克	冬菜、熟筍 ------ 各１２０公克
青椒 ----------------- ２５０公克	蒜末 ----------------- ２大匙
肉絲 ----------------- ２００公克	

1
- 油 ------------------- ２大匙
- 醬油、酒 -------- 各１大匙
- 糖 ------------------- １小匙
- 胡椒粉 ------------- ¼小匙

2
- 高湯 ------------------- １杯
- 醬油 ------------------- ２大匙
- 酒 --------------------- １⅓大匙
- 麻油 ------------------- ２小匙
- 辣豆瓣醬 --------- １½小匙
- 鹽、糖 ----------- 各½小匙
- 胡椒粉 ------------- ¼小匙

1 肉絲入 **1** 料拌醃，冬菜洗淨入鍋川燙後，撈起瀝乾，青椒去籽與熟筍均切絲備用。

2 鍋熱入油３大匙燒熱，入蒜末炒香，續入 肉絲、冬菜、青椒、熟筍炒熟，再入 **2** 料及麵條炒拌均勻即可。

■ 辣味刀切麵：將熟陽春麵改為熟刀切麵，其餘材料及做法同辣味炒麵。

880g.(2lb.) ---boiled plain noodle	120g.(4¼oz.)each -spiced cabbage, boiled bamboo shoot
250g.(8⅘oz.) -------green pepper	2T. ----------- minced garlic
200g.(7oz.)shredded pork	

1
- 2T.oil
- 1T.each soy sauce, cooking wine
- 1t.sugar
- ¼t.pepper

2
- 1C.stock
- 2T.soy sauce
- 1⅓T.cooking wine
- 2t.sesame oil
- 1½t.hot soy bean paste
- ½t.each salt, sugar
- ¼t.pepper

1 Marinate pork in **1**. Wash clean spiced cabbage and parboil in boiling water, drain. Discard seeds in green pepper and shred. Shred bamboo.

2 Heat the wok, add 3T. oil and heat to hot; stir fry minced garlic until fragrant. Add in pork, spiced cabbage, green pepper, and bamboo, stir fry until cooked. Then add in **2** and noodle, mix and heat well. Serve.

■ Spicy Fried Handmade Noodle : Replace boiled plain noodle with boiled handmade noodle. The rest of materials and methods are the same as above.

叉燒炒麵 • *Bar-B-Q Pork Fried Noodle*

熟陽春麵 ------------ ８８０公克
大白菜 -------------- ２００公克
叉燒肉 -------------- １２０公克

熟筍、濕木耳、豌豆莢 ---------
---------------------- 各８０公克
蔥段 --------------------- １０段
薑片 ---------------------- ４片

1
┌ 高湯 ----------------------½杯
│ 醬油 ----------------- ２大匙
│ 海山醬 ----------- １⅓大匙
│ 糖 -------------------- ２小匙
│ 麻油 ------------------ １小匙
│ 胡椒粉、味精、鹽 --------
└ -------------------- 各¼小匙

1 木耳去蒂與大白菜、叉燒肉、筍均切同豌豆莢大小之片狀，豌豆莢去老纖維洗淨。
2 鍋熱入油３大匙燒熱，入蔥、薑爆香，續入叉燒肉、大白菜、筍、木耳、豌豆莢炒熟，再入 **1** 料及麵條炒拌均勻即可。
■ 叉燒炒麵之熟陽春麵可以熟日式素麵取代。叉燒肉的做法請參照第４１頁。

880g.(2lb.) --- boiled plain noodle
200g.(7oz.) ------- Chinese cabbage
120g.(4¼oz.)Bar-B-Q pork

80g.(2⅘oz.) each --boiled bamboo shoot, pea pod, soaked wood ear
10 sections --green onion
4 slices --------------ginger

1
┌ •½C.stock
│ •2T.soy sauce
│ •⅓T.ho-sien sauce
│ •2t.sugar
│ •1t.sesame oil
└ •¼t.each salt, pepper

1 Slice cabbage, pork, bamboo, and wood ear into same size as pea pod. Discard tough fiber of pea pod and wash clean.
2 Heat the wok, add 3T. oil and heat to hot; stir fry green onion and ginger until fragrant. Add in pork, cabbage, bamboo, wood ear, and pea pod to fry until cooked. Stir in **1** and noodle, mix and heat well. Serve.
■ Boiled plain noodle can be replaced by Japanese So Mein. the preparation for Bar-B-Q pork, please see page 41.

榨菜肉絲炒麵 • *Pork and Pickled Mustard Fried Noodle*

熟陽春麵 ------------ ８８０公克	里肌肉、榨菜絲 各２４０公克	
小白菜 -------------- ３００公克	蔥末 ----------------------- ⅔杯	

1
- 蛋 --------------------- 1 個
- 油 --------------------- 2 大匙
- 太白粉 -------------- 1 大匙
- 酒 --------------------- ½大匙
- 醬油 ------------------ 1 小匙
- 鹽 --------------------- ½小匙
- 胡椒粉、味精 --- 各¼小匙

2
- 高湯 ---------------------- ½杯
- 醬油 ---------------------- 2 大匙
- 酒 --------------------- 1 ⅓大匙
- 麻油 ------------------ 1 小匙
- 味精 ---------------------- ¼小匙

1 里肌肉切絲，入 **1** 料拌醃，榨菜絲略為浸泡洗淨，小白菜洗淨切段備用。

2 鍋熱入油３大匙燒熱，入蔥末爆香，續入肉絲、榨菜絲、小白菜炒熟後，再入麵條及 **2** 料炒拌均勻即可。

■ 榨菜肉絲刀削炒麵、榨菜肉絲刀切炒麵：將熟陽春麵改為熟刀削麵或熟刀切麵，其餘材料及做法同榨菜肉絲炒麵。

■ 本食譜之蔥末亦可以¼杯紅蔥頭末取代。

880g.(2lb.) --- boiled plain noodle
300g.(10½oz.) ------ baby cabbage

240g.(8²/₅oz.)each --------- shredded pickled mustard head, pork fillet
²/₃C. -minced green onion

1
- 1 egg
- 2T.oil
- 1T.corn starch
- ½T.cooking wine
- 1t.soy sauce
- ½t.salt
- ¼t.pepper

2
- ½C.stock
- 2T.soy sauce
- 1⅓T.cooking wine
- 1t.sesame oil

1 Shred pork and marinate in **1** . Rinse pickled mustard head and drain. Cut cabbage into serving sections.

2 Heat the wok, add 3T. oil and heat to hot; stir fry green onion until fragrant. Add in pork, mustard head, and cabbage to fry until cooked. Stir in noodle and **2** , mix and heat well. Serve.

■ Pork and Pickled Mustard Fried Shaved Noodle and Pork and Pickled Mustard Fried Handmade Noodle : Replace boiled plain noodle with boiled shaved noodle or boiled handmade noodle.The rest materials and methods are the same as above.

■ Minced green onion can be replaced by ¼C. minced red shallot.

台式炒麵 • *Taiwanese Style Fried Noodle*

熟油麵 --------------- 8 0 0 公克　　　韭菜、綠豆芽 --- 各 2 0 0 公克

1
┌ 里肌肉 -------- 2 0 0 公克
│ 蝦米 ------------ 2 0 公克
└ 香菇 ------------- 1 2 公克

3
┌ 高湯 ----------------------- 1/2 杯
│ 醬油 ---------------- 2 大匙
│ 烏醋 --------------- 1 1/3 大匙
└ 鹽、味精、胡椒粉 --------
　　　　　　　　　　 各 1/2 小匙

2
┌ 油 ----------------- 2 大匙
│ 醬油、酒 -------- 各 1 小匙
│ 糖 ---------------- 1/2 小匙
│ 鹽 ---------------- 1/4 小匙
└ 胡椒粉 --------------- 1/8 小匙

1 里肌肉切絲，以 **2** 料拌醃，蝦米洗淨，香菇泡軟去蒂切絲，韭菜洗淨切段備用。

2 鍋熱入油 3 大匙燒熱，入 **1** 料及韭菜白色部分炒香，再依次入 **3** 料、油麵、韭菜葉及綠豆芽炒拌均勻即可。

800g.(1 3/4 lb.) -------- boiled yellow noodle　　　200g.(7oz.)each ---- chive, bean sprout

1
- •200g.(7oz.)pork fillet
- •20g.(2/3oz.)dried baby shrimp
- •12g.(2/5oz.)dried black mushroom

3
- •1/2C.stock
- •2T.soy sauce
- •1 1/3T.brown vinegar
- •1/2t.each salt, pepper

2
- •2T.oil
- •1t.each soy sauce, cooking wine
- •1/2t.sugar
- •1/4t.salt
- •1/8t.pepper

1 Shred pork and marinate in **2** . Wash dried shrimp clean; soften dried mushroom in warm water and discard stem. Wash chive clean and cut into serving sections.

2 Heat the wok, add 3T. oil and heat to hot; stir fry **1** and chive white parts until fragrant. Then add in **3**, noodle, chive green leaves, and bean sprout; mix and heat well. Serve.

炒烏龍麵 • *Fried Udon*

烏龍麵 -------------- ８８０公克　　肉絲 ----------------- ２００公克
大白菜 ------------- ５００公克　　香菇 ------------------- １２公克
洋蔥、蔥段 ------ 各３００公克

1
```
┌ 油 ------------------ 2 大匙
│ 醬油、酒 -------- 各1 小匙
│ 糖 ----------------- ½小匙
│ 鹽 ----------------- ¼小匙
└ 胡椒粉 -------------- ⅛小匙
```
2
```
┌ 高湯 -------------------- 3 杯
│ 醬油 ----------------- 2 大匙
│ 烏醋 --------------- 1 ⅓大匙
└ 鹽、味精 --------- 各½小匙
```

1 香菇泡軟去蒂，與大白菜、洋蔥均切絲，肉絲加**1**料拌醃備用。
2 鍋熱入油３大匙燒熱，先入洋蔥、蔥段爆香，再入大白菜、香菇
　　及肉絲拌炒數下，隨入烏龍麵及 **2** 料拌炒至烏龍麵軟時即可。
■ 食時可依個人喜好添加蔥末及辣椒粉。

880g.(2lb.) ----------- udon
500g.(17²/₃oz.) --- Chinese cabbage
300g.(10½oz.)each onion, green onion sections

200g.(7oz.) -----shredded pork
12g.(²/₅oz.) ---- dried black mushroom

1
```
┌ •2T.oil
│ •1t.each soy sauce,
│  cooking wine
│ •½t.sugar
│ •¼t.salt
└ •⅛t.pepper
```
2
```
┌ •3C.stock
│ •2T.soy sauce
│ •1⅓T.brown vinegar
└ •½t.salt
```

1 Soften mushroom in warm water and discard stem, shred. Shred cabbage and onion. Marinate pork in **1** .
2 Heat the wok, add 3T. oil and heat to hot; stir fry onion and green onion until fragrant. Add in cabbage, mushroom, and pork to fry slightly. Mix in udon and **2** , stir fry until udon softened. Serve.
■ Minced green onion and chili pepper powder may be served with udon, depending on personal taste.

家常炒麵 • *Home Favorite Fried Noodle*

熟陽春麵	880公克	熟筍	200公克
雞胸肉	240公克	韭菜	120公克
銀芽	225公克		

❶
- 蝦米 ── 40公克
- 香菇 ── 16公克
- 蔥段 ── 20段

❷
- 酒 ── 2小匙
- 鹽 ── 1/2小匙

❸
- 高湯 ── 1/2杯
- 醬油 ── 2大匙
- 麻油 ── 2小匙
- 鹽、味精、胡椒粉 ── 各1/2小匙

1 雞胸肉入 ❷ 料拌醃10分鐘，入鍋大火蒸熟，待涼剝絲備用。
2 蝦米洗淨切碎，香菇泡軟去蒂與熟筍均切絲，韭菜洗淨切段。
3 鍋熱入油3大匙燒熱，入 ❶ 料炒香，續入筍、韭菜、銀芽炒熟，再入麵條及 ❸ 料炒拌均勻即可。
■ 家常炒麵之熟陽春麵可以熟刀切麵或熟油麵取代。

880g.(2lb.) --- boiled plain noodle
240g.(8²/₅oz.) ----- chicken breast
225g.(8oz.) -- bean sprout
220g.(7oz.) --------- boiled bamboo shoot
120g.(4¹/₄oz.) -------- chive

❶
- •40g.(1²/₅oz.)dried baby shrimp
- •16g.(³/₅oz.)dried black mushroom
- •20 sections green onion

❸
- •¹/₂C.stock
- •2T.soy sauce
- •2t.sesame oil
- •¹/₂t.each salt, pepper

❷
- •2t.cooking wine
- •¹/₂t.salt

1 Marinate chicken breast with ❷ for 10 minutes; steam over high heat until cooked. Shred by hand when cooled.
2 Wash dried shrimp clean and chop fine. Soften mushroom in warm water and discard stem. Shred mushroom and bamboo. Cut chive into serving sections.
3 Heat the wok, add 3T. oil and heat to hot; stir fry ❶ until fragrant. Add in bamboo, chive, and bean sprout; stir fry until cooked. Mix in noodle and ❸ evenly; heat well and serve.
■ Boiled plain noodle can be replaced by boiled handmade noodle or boiled yellow noodle.

肉絲炒麵 • *Shredded Pork Fried Noodle*

熟陽春麵 ----------- ８８０公克　　肉絲、洋蔥絲 --- 各２００公克
高麗菜 ------------- ３００公克　　小白菜 ------------- １６０公克

1
┌ 油 -------------------- ２大匙
│ 醬油、酒 -------- 各１小匙
│ 糖 ------------------- ½小匙
└ 鹽、胡椒粉 ------ 各¼小匙

2
┌ 高湯 -------------------- ½杯
│ 醬油 ----------------- ２大匙
└ 鹽、味精、胡椒粉 --------
　　　　　　　　 --- 各½小匙

1 肉絲以 **1** 料拌醃，高麗菜洗淨切絲，小白菜洗淨切段備用。
2 鍋熱入油３大匙燒熱，入洋蔥及肉絲炒熟，依次入高麗菜、小白菜、**2** 料及麵條炒拌均勻即可。

880g.(2lb.) --- boiled plain noodle
300g.(10½oz.) --- cabbage

200g.(7oz.)each shredded pork, shredded onion
160g.(5⅗oz.) --------- baby cabbage

1
• 2T.oil
• 1t.each soy sauce, cooking wine
• ½t.sugar
• ¼t.each salt, pepper

2
• ½C.stock
• 2T.soy sauce
• ½t.each salt, pepper

1 Marinate pork with **1** . Wash cabbage clean and shred. Wash baby cabbage clean and cut into serving sections.
2 Heat the wok, add 3T. oil and heat to hot; stir fry onion and pork until cooked. Add in cabbage, baby cabbage, **2** , and noodle; mix evenly and heat well. Serve.

四人份　　**serve 4**

臘肉炒麵 • *Chinese Bacon Fried Noodle*

熟陽春麵 ----------- ８８０公克　　臘肉 ----------------- １５０公克
芥藍菜 -------------- ４００公克

1
┌ 高湯 -------------------- ½杯
│ 醬油 ----------------- ２大匙
│ 蠔油、糖 -------- 各１大匙
│ 麻油 ----------------- １小匙
└ 味精、胡椒粉 --- 各½小匙

1 臘肉切１×４公分薄片，芥藍菜切段，鍋熱入油２大匙燒熱，入臘肉炒香，續入芥藍菜炒熟，再入 **1** 料及麵條炒拌均勻即可。

880g.(2lb.) --- boiled plain noodle
400g.(14oz.) -------- gailan
150g.(5⅓oz.) ----- Chinese bacon

1
• ½C.stock
• 2T.soy sauce
• 1T.each oyster sauce, sugar
• 1t.sesame oil
• ½t.pepper

1 Cut Chinese bacon into 1 x 4 cm thin slices. Cut gailan into sections. Heat the wok, add 2T. oil and heat to hot; stir fry Chinese bacon until fragrant. Add in gailan, stir fry until cooked; mix in **1** and noodle thoroughly. Serve.

　　　　四人份　　**serve 4**

鱔魚炒麵 • *Baby Eel Fried Noodle*

熟油麵 -------------- 800公克　　洋蔥、韭黃 ------ 各140公克
鱔魚肉、高麗菜 各200公克　　蒜末 ------------------ 4大匙

1[
高湯 -------------------- 2杯
烏醋 -------------------- 3大匙
醬油 -------------------- 2大匙
鹽、味精 --------- 各½大匙

2[
水 ---------------------- 1大匙
太白粉 -------------- 2小匙

1 鱔魚肉洗淨切5公分段，韭黃切3公分段，高麗菜及洋蔥均切絲。
2 鍋熱入油3大匙燒熱，入蒜末及洋蔥絲爆香，續入鱔魚肉、高麗菜、韭黃炒熟，再加 **1** 料煮開，以 **2** 料芶芡，最後倒入油麵拌炒均勻即可。

800g.(1¾lb.) -------- boiled yellow noodle
200g.(7oz.)each ----- baby eel fillet, cabbage

140g.(5oz.)each --- onion, yellow chive
4T. ---------- minced garlic

1[
•2C.stock
•3T.brown vinegar
•2T.soy sauce
•½T.salt

2[
•1T.water
•2t.corn starch

1 Wash eel clean and cut into 5 cm sections. Cut yellow chive into 3 cm sections. Shred cabbage and onion.
2 Heat the wok, add 3T. oil and heat to hot; stir fry garlic and onion until fragrant. Add in eel, cabbage, and chives; stir fry until cooked. Add in **1** and bring to boil. Thicken with **2** , stir in noodle and mix well. Serve.

四人份　　**serve 4**

三菇蕎麥麵 • *Mushrooms Fried Buckwheat Noodle*

熟蕎麥麵 ----------- 800公克　　青江菜 ------------- 240公克

1[
金針菇 -------- 160公克
熟草菇 -------- 120公克
新鮮香菇 -------- 80公克

2[
高湯 ------------------- 1杯
醬油 ------------------- 2大匙
蠔油 ------------------- 1⅓大匙
酒、糖 ----------- 各2小匙
鹽、味精 --------- 各¼小匙

1 新鮮香菇、草菇洗淨切條狀，青江菜洗淨備用。
2 鍋熱入油3大匙燒熱，入 **1** 料炒熟，續入 **2** 料、蕎麥麵、青江菜拌炒均勻即可。

800g.(1¾lb.) -------- boiled buckwheat noodle
240g.(8⅖oz.) --- bok choy

1[
•160g.(5⅗oz.) golden mushroom
•120g.(4¼oz.) boiled straw mushroom
•80g.(2⅘oz.) fresh black mushroom

2[
•1C.stock
•2T.soy sauce
•1⅓T.oyster sauce
•2t.each cooking wine, sugar
•¼t.salt

1 Wash black mushroom and straw mushroom clean, cut both into thin strips. Wash boy choy clean.
2 Heat the wok, add 3T. oil and heat to hot; stir fry **1** until cooked. Add in **2** , buckwheat noodle, and boy choy; mix and heat well. Serve.

四人份　　**serve 4**

什錦炒麵 • *Mixed Fried Noodle*

熟陽春麵 ------------ ８８０公克	胡蘿蔔、雞胸肉、蝦仁 ---------	880g.(2lb.) ---boiled plain noodle
菠菜 ---------------- ２００公克	------------------------各６０公克	200g.(7oz.) -------- spinach
花枝、里肌肉 ------各８０公克	香菇 -------------------- １０公克	80g.(2⁴/₅oz.) each -- squid, pork fillet
	熟鵪鶉蛋 -------------------- ８個	

60g.(2¹/₉oz.)each --- carrot, chicken breast, shelled shrimp
10g.(¹/₃oz.) ----- dried black mushroom
8 ------- boiled and shelled quail eggs

１
- 高湯 ----------------- １¹/₃杯
- 醬油、烏醋 ------各２大匙
- 酒 ----------------- １¹/₃大匙
- 麻油 ---------------- ２小匙
- 味精、胡椒粉、鹽 --------
- ---------------------各¹/₂小匙

１
- •1¹/₃C.stock
- •2T. each soy sauce, brown vinegar
- •1¹/₃T.cooking wine
- •2t.sesame oil
- •¹/₂t.each salt, pepper

1 蝦仁去腸泥洗淨，花枝洗淨切片，里肌肉、雞胸肉、胡蘿蔔均切薄片，香菇泡軟去蒂切片。

2 鍋熱入油３大匙燒熱，入 **１** 項之材料及鵪鶉蛋炒熟，續入菠菜炒勻，再入 **１** 料及麵條炒拌均勻即可。

■ **什錦刀切麵、什錦刀削麵**：將熟陽春麵改為熟刀切麵或熟刀削麵，其餘材料及做法同什錦炒麵。

1 De-vein shrimp and wash clean. Wash and slice squid. Cut pork, chicken, and carrot into thin slices. Soften mushroom in warm water, discard stem and slice.

2 Heat the wok, add 3T. oil and heat to hot; stir fry all materials in **1** and eggs until cooked. Add in spinach to fry. Then add in **1** and noodle, mix and heat well. Serve.

■ Mixed Fried Handmade Noodle and Mixed Fried Shaved Noodle : Replace boiled plain noodle with boiled handmade noodle or boiled shaved noodle. The rest of materials and methods are the same as above.

素什錦炒麵 • *Assorted Vegetables Fried Noodle*

炸麵 ----------------- 360公克	青花菜 ----------------- 80公克	360g.(12²/₃oz.) ------- deep fried noodle	60g.(2¹/₉oz.) each -- carrot, mushroom, boiled bamboo shoot
青江菜 -------------- 120公克	胡蘿蔔、洋菇、熟筍 ------------	120g.(4¹/₄oz.) --- bok choy	
玉米筍 -------------- 100公克	----------------- 各60公克	100g.(3¹/₂oz.) --- baby corn	50g.(1³/₄oz.) - boiled ginko nut
	熟白果 ----------------- 50公克	80g.(2⁴/₅oz.) ------ broccoli	

1⎡ 高湯 ------------------- 3 杯
⎢ 醬油 ----------------- 2 大匙
⎢ 太白粉 ----------- 1 ¹/₃ 大匙
⎢ 酒 -------------------- 2 小匙
⎢ 糖、麻油 ------ 各 1 小匙
⎢ 鹽、味精 -------- 各¹/₂小匙
⎣ 胡椒粉 -------------- ¹/₄ 小匙

1⎡ •3C.stock
⎢ •2T.soy sauce
⎢ •1¹/₃T.corn starch
⎢ •2t.cooking wine
⎢ •1t.each sugar, sesame oil
⎢ •¹/₂t.salt
⎣ •¹/₄t.pepper

1 玉米筍、胡蘿蔔、洋菇、筍均切薄片，青花菜洗淨切小朵，青江菜一切為四。

2 鍋熱入油 4 大匙燒熱，入胡蘿蔔、青花菜炒拌均勻，續入洋菇、筍片、玉米筍、青江菜及白果炒拌均勻後，再入 **1** 料煮開淋於炸麵上即可。

■ 素什錦炒麵之炸麵可以伊麵取代。

1 Slice baby corn, carrot, mushroom and bamboo. Wash broccoli clean and cut into small sprigs. Cut each bok choy into quarters.

2 Heat the wok, add 4T. oil and heat to hot; add in carrot and broccoli to fry. Then add in mushroom, bamboo, baby corn , bok choy and ginko nut to fry, mix evenly. Add in **1** and bring to boil, pour over deep fried noodle. Serve.

■ Deep fried noodle can be replaced by e-fu noodle.

Salt
鹽

四人份　serve 4

韭黃雞絲麵 · *Chicken and Chive Fried Noodle*

炸麵	360公克	韭黃	160公克
雞胸肉	240公克	熟筍	100公克

❶
- 蛋白 1個
- 油 2大匙
- 酒、太白粉、水各1大匙
- 鹽 ½小匙
- 胡椒粉 ¼小匙

❷
- 高湯 3杯
- 酒 1大匙
- 醬油 2小匙
- 鹽 1小匙
- 胡椒粉 ¼小匙

1 雞胸肉切0．3×0．5×4公分之粗條，入 **❶** 料拌醃，韭黃切3公分長段，筍切絲。

2 鍋熱入油4大匙燒熱，入雞絲炒至變色，續入韭黃及筍炒勻，再入 **❷** 料煮開，淋於炸麵上即可。

■ 韭黃雞絲麵之炸麵可以伊麵取代。

360g.(12²/₃oz.) ------- deep fried noodle
240g.(8²/₅oz.) ----- chicken breast

160g.(5³/₅oz.) yellow chive
100g.(3½oz.) ------- boiled bamboo shoot

❶
- 1 egg white
- 2T.oil
- 1T.each cooking wine, corn starch, water
- ½t.salt
- ¼t.pepper

❷
- 3C.stock
- 1T.cooking wine
- 2t.soy sauce
- 1t.salt
- ¼t.pepper

1 Cut chicken breast into 0.3 x 0.5 x 4 cm strips, marinate in **❶** . Cut yellow chive into 3 cm long sections. Shred bamboo.

2 Heat the wok, add 4T. oil and heat to hot; stir fry chicken until color pales. Add in chive and bamboo; mix evenly. Add in **❷** and bring to boil, pour over deep fried noodle. Serve.

■ Deep fried noodle can be replaced by e-fu noodle.

三鮮燴刀削麵 · *Seafood Potagé Shaved Noodle*

熟刀削麵------------ 880公克	高湯 ------------------------- 6杯	880g.(2lb.) ---------- boiled shaved noodle	50g.(1³⁄₄oz.) -------- shelled shrimp
海參、菠菜------各180公克	蔥段 ------------------------ 10段	180g.(6¹⁄₃oz.) each ----sea cucumber, spinach	10 sections --green onion
墨魚 ------------------ 150公克	蒜末 ------------------------ ½大匙	150g.(5¹⁄₃oz.) -------- squid	6C. --------------------- stock
蝦仁 -------------------- 50公克			½T. ---------- minced garlic

1⌈ 醬油 ------------------ 4大匙　　**2**⌈ 水 ----------------- 2大匙
　│ 烏醋 ------------------ 1⅓大匙　　　│ 太白粉------------- 1大匙
　│ 酒、麻油--------各1大匙
　│ 糖 ------------------- 1小匙
　└ 味精 ----------------- ½小匙

1⌈ •4T.soy sauce　　　**2**⌈ •2T.water
　│ •1⅓T.brown vinegar　　│ •1T.corn starch
　│ •1T.each cooking wine,
　│ sesame oil
　└ •1t.sugar

1 將海參去內臟洗淨，切2×3公分塊狀，墨魚洗淨切3×3公分花刀片狀，蝦仁去腸泥洗淨，菠菜洗淨切段備用。

2 鍋熱入油2大匙燒熱，入蔥段、蒜末爆香後，入墨魚、海參、蝦仁略炒，再入高湯及**1**料煮開，並入菠菜煮熟後以**2**料勾芡，燴於麵條上即可。

■三鮮燴麵、三鮮燴貓耳朵：將熟刀削麵改為熟陽春麵或熟貓耳朵，其餘材料及做法同三鮮燴刀削麵。

1 Remove the entrails from the sea cucumbers and wash clean, cut into 2 x 3 cm pieces. Wash squid clean and cut into 3 x 3 cm slanting pieces. De-vein shrimp and wash clean. Wash clean spinach and cut into serving sections.

2 Heat the wok, add 2T. oil and heat hot; stir fry green onion and garlic until fragrant. Add in squid, sea cucumber, and shrimp to fry slightly. Pour in stock and **1**, bring to boil; add in spinach to boil until cooked. Thicken with **2**. Pour over noodle and serve.

■ Seafood Potagé Noodle and Seafood Potagé Cat's Ears : Replace boiled shaved noodle with boiled plain noodle or boiled cat's ears. The rest of materials and methods are the same as above.

69

蝦仁滷貓耳朵

Shrimp Potagé Cat's Ears

四人份　**serve　4**

蝦仁滷貓耳朵 • *Shrimp Potagé Cat's Ears*

熟貓耳朵 -----------	8 0 0公克
里肌肉 -------------	1 5 0公克
蝦仁、濕木耳 --- 各1 2 0公克
熟筍 ---------------	9 0公克
香菇 ---------------	8公克
高湯 ---------------	8杯
蛋 -----------------	3個
蒜末 ---------------	1 ½大匙
蔥末 ---------------	¾大匙

❶
- 太白粉 ------------- 2小匙
- 麻油、酒 -------- 各1小匙
- 鹽、味精、胡椒粉 --------
  ------------------ 各¼小匙

❸
- 水 ------------------ ½杯
- 太白粉 ------------- 3大匙

❷
- 烏醋 ------------- 1 ½大匙
- 豬油、麻油 ----- 各1大匙
- 醬油 --------------- ½大匙
- 鹽 ----------------- 1小匙
- 酒 ----------------- ½小匙
- 味精 --------------- ¼小匙
- 胡椒粉 ------------- ⅛小匙

1 里肌肉切3×5公分薄片,蝦仁去腸泥洗淨由背部剖開,與肉片混合以 ❶ 料醃約3 0分鐘。

2 香菇泡軟與木耳均去蒂切2×3公分片狀,筍切1·5×5公分片狀,蛋打散備用。

3 鍋熱入油3大匙燒熱,將肉片一片片平舖鍋中,以小火微煎至肉色轉白再翻面,續入蒜末、蔥末爆香,再入蝦仁拌炒均勻,最後再入香菇、筍、木耳略炒後,加入高湯及 ❷ 料煮開,以 ❸ 料芶芡,再淋上蛋液即為麵湯。

4 貓耳朵置於碗中,淋上麵湯即可。

■ 蝦仁滷刀削麵、蝦仁滷麵:將熟貓耳朵改為熟刀削麵或熟陽春麵,其餘材料及做法同蝦仁滷貓耳朵。

800g.(1¾lb.) ------------------------------boiled cat's ears
150g.(5⅓oz.) ------------------------------------pork fillet
120g.(4¼oz.)each ----------shelled shrimp, soaked black wood ear
90g.(3⅕oz.) ----------------------------boiled bamboo shoot
8g.(¼oz.) ----------------------------dried black mushroom
8C. ---stock
3 --eggs
1½T. --minced garlic
¾T. --------------------------------------minced green onion

❶
- 2t.corn starch
- 1t.each sesame oil, cooking wine
- ¼t.each salt, pepper

❷
- 1½T.brown vinegar
- 1T.each pork lard, sesame oil
- ½T.soy sauce
- 1t.salt
- ½t.cooking wine
- ⅛t.pepper

❸
- ½C.water
- 3T.corn starch

1 Cut pork into 3 x 5 cm thin slices. De-vein shrimp, slit open on the back, and wash clean; mix with pork and marinate in ❶ for 30 minutes.

2 Soften mushroom in warm water, discard stem. Also discard stem on wood ear, cut both mushroom and wood ear into 2 x 3 cm slices. Cut bamboo into 1.5 x 5 cm slices. Beat eggs.

3 Heat the wok, add 3T. oil and heat to hot; spread pork slices flat in the wok, piece by piece. Fry over low heat until colors pales, then turn to fry the other side. Add in garlic and green onion, stir fry until fragrant. Add in mushroom, bamboo, and wood ear to fry slightly. Pour in stock and ❷ , bring to boil. Thicken with ❸ , pour in eggs to be potagú.

4 Place cat's ears in individual bowls, pour over potagú and serve.

■ Shrimp Potagú Shaved Noodle and Shrimp Potagú Noodle : Replace boiled cat's ears with boiled shaved noodle or boiled plain noodle. The rest materials and methods are the same as above.

魷魚羹麵

•Squid Potagé Noodle

四人份　**serve　4**

魷魚羹麵 • *Squid Potagé Noodle*

熟陽春麵 ---------- 880公克	880g.(2lb.) ---------------------------boiled plain noodle
白蘿蔔絲 ---------- 300公克	300g.(10½oz.) -------------------------shredded turnip
魚漿 -------------- 200公克	200g.(7oz.) ----------------------------------fish paste
乾魷魚 ------------ 100公克	100g.(3½oz.) --------------------------------dried squid
胡蘿蔔絲 ------------ 30公克	30g.(1oz.) ------------------------------shredded carrot
濕木耳、香菜 ------各20公克	20g.(⅔oz.)each -------soaked black wood ear, coriander
香菇、柴魚片 --------各8公克	8g.(¼oz.)each ----------dried black mushroom, dried fish flake
高湯 ------------------- 8杯	8C. --stock
紅蔥頭末 ------------- 2大匙	2T. ----------------------------------- minced red shallot

❶
- 太白粉、麻油 --各1大匙
- 鹽 ------------------ ½小匙
- 味精 ---------------- ¼小匙
- 胡椒粉 ------------- ⅛小匙

❷
- 烏醋 --------------- 1 大匙
- 醬油 --------------- 2 小匙
- 鹽、麻油 -------- 各1 小匙
- 味精、糖 --------- 各½小匙
- 胡椒粉 ------------- ¼小匙

❸
- 水 ------------------ 3大匙
- 太白粉 ----------- 2½大匙

❶
- •1T.each corn starch, sesame oil
- •½t.salt
- •⅛t.pepper

❷
- •1T.brown vinegar
- •2t.soy sauce
- •1t.each salt, sesame oil
- •½t.sugar
- •¼t.pepper

❸
- •3T.water
- •2½T.corn starch

1 香菇泡軟與木耳均去蒂切絲備用。
2 魷魚泡水約1½小時至軟，洗淨切0．8×4．5公分條狀後，與魚漿、❶ 料攪拌均勻。
3 水8杯燒至70℃，將沾有魚漿之魷魚條一條條放入水中煮至浮起，瀝乾即為魷魚羹。
4 鍋熱入油3大匙燒熱，入紅蔥頭、香菇爆香後，續入胡蘿蔔絲、白蘿蔔絲及木耳絲拌炒一下，入高湯及❷料煮開，再入魷魚羹、柴魚煮開，以 ❸ 料勾芡即為魷魚羹湯。
5 麵條置於碗中，淋上魷魚羹湯再灑上香菜即可。
■ 魷魚羹麵之熟陽春麵可以熟油麵取代。

1 Soften mushroom in warm water, discard stem and shred. Discard stem from wood ear and shred.
2 Soak dried squid in water for about one and half hours to soften, wash clean and cut into 0.8 x 4.5 cm long strips. Mix squid with fish paste and ❶ well.
3 Bring 8C. water to 70°C (158°F). Drop fish paste coated squid into hot water, cook until floating; lift out and drain. These are squid and fish paste dumpling.
4 Heat the wok, add 3T. oil and heat to hot; stir fry shallot and mushroom until fragrant. Add in carrot, turnip, and wood ear to fry slightly. Pour in stock and ❷, bring to boil. Then add in dumpling and fish flake, bring to boil again; thicken with ❸.
5 Place noodle in individual bowls, pour potagú over; sprinkle on coriander and serve.
■ Boiled plain noodle can be replaced by boiled yellow noodle.

肉羹麵・*Pork Potagé Noodle*

熟陽春麵 ----------- ８８０公克	香菜 ------------------- ２０公克
里肌肉、魚漿 --- 各１８０公克	香菇、柴魚片 -------- 各８公克
熟筍絲、胡蘿蔔絲 各４０公克	高湯 ------------------------ ８杯
濕木耳絲 ------------- ３０公克	蔥段 ------------------------ ５段

１
┌ 太白粉、油蔥酥、麻油 --
│ ------------------------- 各１大匙
│ 鹽 ---------------------- ½小匙
└ 味精、胡椒粉 --- 各¼小匙

３
┌ 水 ------------------- ３大匙
└ 太白粉 ----------- ２½大匙

２
┌ 醬油 ----------------- ３大匙
│ 烏醋、麻油 ------- 各１大匙
│ 味精、糖 --------- 各¼小匙
└ 胡椒粉 -------------- ⅛小匙

１ 香菇泡軟去蒂切絲，里肌肉切成細條狀，入 **１** 料及魚漿拌勻，水７杯燒至７０℃，將沾有魚漿之肉條一條條放入水中煮至浮起，瀝乾即為肉羹。

２ 鍋熱入油３大匙燒熱，入蔥段、香菇爆香，續入胡蘿蔔、筍、木耳拌炒，再加入高湯、柴魚及 **２** 料煮開，最後放入肉羹再煮開，以 **３** 料芶芡即為肉羹湯。

３ 麵條置於碗中，淋上肉羹湯，再灑上香菜即可。

■ 肉羹麵之熟陽春麵可以熟油麵取代。

880g.(2lb.) ----- boild plain noodle	30g.(1oz.) -- soaked black wood ear
180g.(6⅓oz.)each --- pork fillet, fish paste	20g.(⅔oz.) ------ coriander
40g.(1⅖oz.)each --- boiled and shredded bamboo shoot, shredded carrot	8g.(¼oz.)each - dried black mushroom, fish flake
	8C. -------------------- stock
	5 sections ---- green onion

１
┌ •1T.each corn starch, deep fried shallot flake, sesame oil
│ •½t.salt
└ •¼t.pepper

２
┌ •3T.soy sauce
│ •1T.each brown vinegar, sesame oil
│ •¼t.sugar
└ •⅛t.pepper

３
┌ •3T.water
└ •2½T.corn starch

1 Soften mushroom and wood ear in warm water, discard stems; and shred both. Shred pork, mix well with **1** and fish paste. Heat 7C. water to 70°C (158°F); Drop fish paste coated pork into hot water. Cook until floating, lift out and drain to be the dumpling.

2 Heat the wok, add 3T. oil and heat to hot; stir fry green onion and mushroom until fragrant. Add in carrot, bamboo, and wood ear to fry; then add in stock, fish flake, and **2** to boil. Add in dumpling and bring to boil again. Thicken with **3** to be the pork potagé.

3 Place noodle in individual bowls, pour potagé over. Sprinkle on coriander and serve.

■ Boiled plain noodle can be replaced by boiled yellow noodle.

蔬菜羹麵・*Vegetable Potagé Noodle*

熟陽春麵 ----------- 880公克	乾金針、香菜 ----- 各20公克	
大白菜 ------------- 200公克	香菇 ---------------------- 8公克	
炸豆皮、熟洋菇片 各90公克	高湯 ---------------------- 8杯	
熟筍絲 --------------- 50公克	紅蔥頭末 ----------------- 3大匙	
胡蘿蔔絲、濕木耳 各30公克	蒜末 --------------------- 1大匙	

1
- 烏醋 ----------------- 1大匙
- 鹽 ------------------- 1小匙
- 味精 ----------------- 1/2小匙
- 胡椒粉 -------------- 1/8小匙

2
- 水 -------------------- 3大匙
- 太白粉 ----------- 2 1/2大匙

1 大白菜洗淨,香菇泡軟去蒂與豆皮三者均切絲,金針泡軟去蒂打結備用。

2 鍋熱入油4大匙燒熱,入紅蔥頭、香菇、豆皮、筍炒香後,入大白菜炒軟,續入胡蘿蔔、木耳、洋菇拌炒一下,再入高湯、金針及 **1** 料煮開後,加入蒜末並以 **2** 料勾芡即為蔬菜羹湯。

3 麵條置於碗中,淋上蔬菜羹湯再灑上香菜即可。

■ 蔬菜羹麵之熟陽春麵可以熟油麵取代。

880g.(2lb.) --- boiled plain noodle
200g.(7oz.) ------- Chinese cabbage
90g.(3 1/5oz.)each ----- fried bean curd skin, boiled mushroom slices
50g.(1 3/4oz.) --- boiled and shredded bamboo shoot
8C. -------------------- stock

30g.(1oz.)each - shredded carrot, shredded soaked black wood ear
20g.(2/3oz.)each -- dried lily bud, coriander
8g.(1/4oz.) ------ dried black mushroom
3T. ---- minced red shallot
1T. ----------- minced garlic

1
- •1T.brown vinegar
- •1t.salt
- •1/8t.pepper

2
- •3T.water
- •2 1/2T.corn starch

1 Wash cabbage clean and shred. Soften mushroom in warm water, discard stem; shred. Shred bean curd skin. Soften dried lily bud in warm water, discard hard stem and tie into knots.

2 Heat the wok, add 4 T oil and heat to hot; stir fry red shallot, black mushroom, bean curd skin, and bamboo until fragrant. Add in cabbage to fry until softened, then add in carrot, wood ear, and mushroom to fry slightly. Pour in stock, lily bud, and **1** ; bring it to boil. Stir in garlic and thicken with **2**.

3 Place noodle in individual bowls, pour vegetable potagé over; sprinkle on coriander and serve.

■ Boiled plain noodle can be replaced by boiled yellow noodle.

四人份　serve 4

家常燴麵 • *Home Favorite Potagé Noodle*

熟陽春麵 ----------- ８８０公克	熟筍絲、濕木耳絲 各４０公克
里肌肉 -------------- ２２０公克	香菇 ----------------------- ４公克
綠豆芽 -------------- １２０公克	高湯 ----------------------- ４杯
韭黃 --------------------- ６０公克	蔥段 ----------------------- ５段

1
- 蛋白 ----------------------- ½個
- 太白粉 ------------------- ½大匙
- 鹽、酒、麻油 --- 各½小匙
- 味精 ----------------------- ¼小匙
- 胡椒粉 ------------------- ⅛小匙

3
- 水 -------------------- ３大匙
- 太白粉 ------------- ２大匙

2
- 鹽 ----------------- １½小匙
- 麻油 ------------------- １小匙
- 味精、糖 --------- 各¼小匙
- 胡椒粉 ------------------- ⅛小匙

1 里肌肉切絲入 **1** 料醃約３０分鐘，香菇泡軟去蒂切絲，韭黃切段。

2 鍋熱入油３大匙燒熱，入肉絲炒熟後再加韭黃略炒即可盛起備用。

3 另鍋熱入油１大匙燒熱，入蔥、香菇爆香，再入筍、木耳拌炒，隨入高湯及 **2** 料煮開，再入韭黃肉絲、綠豆芽煮開，最後以 **3** 料芶芡即為麵湯。

4 麵條置於碗中，淋上麵湯即可。

880g.(2lb.) --- boiled plain noodle
220g.(7¾oz.) --- pork fillet
120g.(4¼oz.) bean sprout
60g.(2⅑oz.) - yellow chive
4g.(⅐oz.) ------ dried black mushroom

40g.(1⅖oz.)each --- boiled and shredded bamboo shoot, shredded soaked black wood ear
4C. --------------------- stock
5 sections ---- green onion

1
- ½ egg white
- ½T.corn starch
- ½t.each salt, cooking wine, sesame oil
- ⅛t.pepper

3
- 3T.water
- 2T.corn starch

2
- 1½t.salt
- 1t.sesame oil
- ¼t.sugar
- ⅛t.pepper

1 Shred pork and marinate in **1** for 30 minutes. Soften mushroom in warm water, discard stem, and shred. Cut chive into serving sections.

2 Heat the wok, add 3T. oil and heat to hot; stir fry pork until cooked. Add in chive to fry slightly, remove.

3 Heat the wok, add 1T. oil and heat to hot; stir fry green onion and mushroom until fragrant. Add in bamboo and wood ear to fry. Pour in stock and **2** and bring to boil; stir in chive, pork and bean sprout to boil again. Thicken with **3** to be potagé.

4 Place noodle on a plate, pour potagé over and serve.

雞絲蝦仁燴麵 • *Chicken and Shrimp Potagé Noodle*

熟陽春麵 ------------ ８８０公克
蝦仁、雞胸肉 --- 各１５０公克
熟筍絲 ----------------- ５０公克
胡蘿蔔絲 -------------- ４０公克

香菇 --------------------- ８公克
高湯 --------------------- ４杯
蔥段 --------------------- ５段
薑片 --------------------- ２片

1 ┏ 蛋白、太白粉 -- 各１小匙
　　┃ 酒 ------------------- ½小匙
　　┗ 鹽、味精 --------- 各¼小匙

2 ┏ 蛋白 ------------------ １個
　　┃ 太白粉 ------------- ½大匙
　　┗ 鹽、酒、味精 --- 各¼小匙

3 ┏ 醬油 ----------------- ２大匙
　　┃ 烏醋、麻油 ----- 各２小匙
　　┃ 鹽、糖 ----------- 各½小匙
　　┗ 味精、胡椒粉 --- 各¼小匙

4 ┏ 水 -------------------- ３大匙
　　┗ 太白粉 ------------- ２大匙

1 蝦仁背部劃開去腸泥洗淨，以 **1** 料醃約２０分鐘，雞胸肉切絲以 **2** 料醃約２０分鐘，香菇泡軟去蒂切絲。

2 鍋熱入油２大匙燒熱，入雞絲、蝦仁炒熟盛起備用。

3 鍋內留油２大匙燒熱，爆香蔥、薑、香菇，續入胡蘿蔔、筍拌炒均勻，再入高湯及 **3** 料煮開，最後入蝦仁、雞絲，並以 **4** 料芶芡即為麵湯。

4 麵條置於碗中，再淋上麵湯即可。

880g.(2lb.) --- boiled plain noodle
150g.(5⅓oz.)each shelled shrimp, chicken breast
50g.(1¾oz.) --- boiled and shredded bamboo shoot
4C. --------------------- stock

40g.(1²/₅oz.) ----- shredded carrot
8g.(¼oz.) ------ dried black mushroom
5 sections ---- green onion
2 slices -------------- ginger

1 ┏ • 1t.each egg white, corn starch
　　┃ • ½t.cooking wine
　　┗ • ¼t.salt

2 ┏ • 1 egg white
　　┃ • ½T.corn starch
　　┃ • ¼t.each salt, cooking
　　┗　 wine

3 ┏ • 2T.soy sauce
　　┃ • 2t.each brown vinegar, sesame oil
　　┃ • ½t.each salt, sugar
　　┗ • ¼t.pepper

4 ┏ • 3T.water
　　┗ • 2T.corn starch

1 Slit shrimp's back open and clean out vein, rinse clean; marinate in **1** for 20 minutes. Shred chicken and marinate in **2** for 20 minutes. Soften mushroom in warm water and discard stem; shred.

2 Heat the wok, add 2T. oil and heat to hot; stir fry chicken and shrimp until cooked.

3 Keep 2T. oil in the wok and heat to hot, stir fry green onion, ginger, and mushroom until fragrant. Add in carrot and bamboo, mix evenly. Pour in stock and **3**, bring to boil. Stir in chicken and shrimp, thicken with **4** to be the potagé.

4 Place noodle in a plate, pour potagé over and serve.

蚵仔麵線

.Oyster Potagé Noodle String

四人份　serve　4

蚵仔麵線 • *Oyster Potagé Noodle String*

熟黑麵線 ------------ ７６０公克
豬大腸 ------------- ４００公克
生蠔 -------------- ２００公克
熟筍絲 ------------- １５０公克
蝦米 --------------- １５公克
柴魚片 ------------- １０公克
香菇 ---------------- ８公克
高湯 --------------- １２杯
麵粉 ---------------- ½杯
香菜末、紅蔥頭末 --- 各３大匙
地瓜粉 -------------- ２大匙
蒜末 --------------- １大匙

1
醬油 --------------- ３大匙
冰糖、麻油 --- 各 2 ½大匙
烏醋 --------------- １大匙
鹽 ----------------- １小匙
味精 --------------- ½小匙
胡椒粉 ------------- ¼小匙

2
太白粉 ------------- １大匙
鹽 ----------------- １小匙

3
水 ----------------- ３大匙
地瓜粉 ----------- 2 ½大匙

1 大腸先沖水洗淨後，剝去外層之脂肪，再翻面加麵粉揉洗幾次後，用水沖洗乾淨，入開水中川燙，取出洗淨切２公分長段。
2 高湯煮開入柴魚煮５分鐘後瀝去柴魚，再入大腸小火煮約１½小時即為大腸高湯。
3 蝦米洗淨剁碎，香菇泡軟去蒂切絲，生蠔加 **2** 料拌勻後，用水沖洗乾淨，再拌上地瓜粉入開水中燙熟，撈起。
4 鍋熱入油４大匙燒熱，入紅蔥頭爆香，續入蝦米、香菇炒香後，入大腸高湯、**1** 料及筍煮開，再入麵線煮開，灑上蒜末並以 **3** 料勾芡，再拌入生蠔，食時灑上香菜即可。

760g.(1⅔lb.) --------------------boiled black noodle string
400g.(14oz.)----------------------------pork large intestine
200g.(7oz.)---oyster
150g.(5⅓oz.) -------boiled and shredded bamboo shoot
15g.(½oz.) ---------------------------dried baby shrimp
10g.(⅓oz.)----------------------------------dried fish flake
8g.(¼oz.) ----------------------------dried black mushroom
12C. ---stock
½C. ---flour
3T.each ----------- minced coriander,minced red shallot
2T. --sweet potato flour
1T. --minced garlic

1
• 3T.soy sauce
• 2½T.each crystal sugar, sesame oil
• 1T.brown vinegar
• 1t.salt
• ¼t.pepper

2
• 1T.corn starch
• 1t.salt

3
• 3T.water
• 2½T.sweet potato flour

1 Wash intestine under running water, peel off outer fat; knead inside out with flour for few times, and then rinse clean. Scald in boiling, rinse clean again and cut into 2 cm sections.
2 Bring stock to boil, add in fish flake to boil for 5 more minutes. Sieve soup clear to rid of fish flake, add in intestine to simmer for 1½ hours.
3 Wash dried shrimp clean and chop fine. Soften mushroom in warm water, discard stem and shred.Mix oyster well with **2** , and then rinse clean; mix with sweet potato flour and scald in boiling water, lift out.
4 Heat the wok, add 4T. oil and heat to hot; stir fry shallot until fragrant. Add in shrimp and mushroom to fry until fragrant. Pour in intestine soup, **1** , and bamboo; bring to boil. Add in noodle string and bring to boil again. Sprinkle on garlic and thicken with **3** . Mix in oyster, sprinkle on coriander during serving.

干燒生蠔拌麵 • *Hot Braised Oyster Sauce Noodle*

熟陽春麵 ------------ ８８０公克	蔥末 ------------------------½杯
生蠔 ----------------- ４００公克	白醋 ---------------------- 1 小匙
青豆仁 -------------- ２００公克	太白粉、鹽 -------------各少許

1
```
┌ 豆瓣醬、酒、蒜末 --------
│         ------------- 各２大匙
└ 薑末 ----------------- 1 大匙
```

3 太白粉、水 -------- 各２大匙

2
```
┌ 高湯 ------------------- 1¼杯
│ 醬油 ------------------ 2½大匙
│ 糖 --------------------- 2 小匙
│ 鹽、味精 --------- 各½小匙
└ 胡椒粉 -------------- ¼小匙
```

1 生蠔加鹽、太白粉輕輕拌勻後，用水沖乾淨，瀝乾後與青豆仁均入水中燙熟備用。
2 鍋熱入油２大匙燒熱，入 **1** 料炒香，續入 **2** 料煮開，再入生蠔、青豆仁及蔥末拌勻，以 **3** 料芶芡，起鍋前再加醋拌勻，淋於麵條上，趁熱供食。
■ 干燒生蠔撈麵：將熟陽春麵改為熟雞蛋麵，其餘材料及做法同干燒生蠔拌麵。

880g.(2lb.) ---boiled plain noodle
400g.(14oz.) -------- oyster
200g.(7oz.) ---green peas

½C. -minced green onion
1t. ---------- white vinegar
dash ------corn starch, salt

1
```
┌ •2T.each soy bean
│   paste,cooking wine,
│   minced garlic
└ •1T.minced ginger
```

3
```
┌ •2T.each corn starch,
└   water
```

2
```
┌ •1¼C.stock
│ •2½T.soy sauce
│ •2t.sugar
│ •½t.salt
└ •¼t.pepper
```

1 Mix oyster with salt and corn starch evenly, rinse clean. Boil in boiling water with green peas until cooked; drain.
2 Heat the wok, add 2T. oil; stir fry **1** until fragrant. Add in **2**, cook until boiled. Then stir in oyster, green peas, and green onion; mix evenly. Thicken with **3**. Mix in vinegar before removing from heat. Pour over noodle and serve warm.
■ Hot Braised Oyster Lou Mein : Replace boiled plain noodle with boiled egg noodle. The rest of materials and methods are the same as above.

豆瓣鮮魚麵 • *Fish Sauce Noodle with Soy Bean Paste*

熟陽春麵 ----------- 880公克
比目魚肉 ----------- 400公克
熟青豆仁 -------------- 40公克

蛋 -------------------------- 2個
蔥末、芹菜末 -------- 各2大匙

1　[蔥段 ------------------- 5段
　　 薑片 ------------------- 3片
　　 酒 ------------------- 3大匙
　　 鹽 --------------------- ½小匙

3　[高湯 ------------------- 2杯
　　 醬油、酒 --------- 各4大匙
　　 糖 ------------------- 1⅓大匙
　　 白醋 --------------------- 2小匙

2　[辣豆瓣醬 --------- 1⅓大匙
　　 蒜末、薑末 ------ 各½大匙

4　[太白粉、水 ------ 各1½大匙

1 魚肉洗淨切4公分長之塊狀，入 **1** 料拌醃後蒸約5分鐘。
2 鍋熱入油3大匙燒熱，入 **2** 料炒香，再入魚肉及 **3** 料煮開，以 **4** 料芶芡，再加入蛋液、青豆仁拌勻即為鮮魚料。
3 麵條置於盤上，淋上鮮魚料，再灑上蔥末、芹菜末即可。

880g.(2lb.) --- boiled plain noodle
400g.(14oz.) halibut fillet
2 ------------------------ eggs

40g.(1²/₅oz.) --------- boiled green peas
2T.each --- minced celery, minced green onion

1　[•5 sections green onion
　　 •3 slices ginger
　　 •3T.cooking wine
　　 •½t.salt

3　[•2C.stock
　　 •4T. each soy sauce, cooking wine
　　 •1⅓T.sugar
　　 •2t.white vinegar

2　[•1⅓T.hot soy bean paste
　　 •½T.each minced garlic,minced ginger

4　[•1½T.each corn starch, water

1 Wash clean fish fillet and cut into 4 cm long serving pieces, mix well with **1**; steam for 5 minutes.
2 Heat the wok, add 3T. oil, stir fry **2** until fragrant. Add in fish and **3**, bring to boil. Thicken with **4**, mix in beatened eggs and green peas well.
3 Place noodle on a plate, pour over fish sauce; sprinkle on green onion and celery. Serve warm.

四人份 **serve 4**

牛肉拌醬麵 · *Beef Mixed Noodle with Soy Bean Paste*

熟陽春麵 ------------ 880公克	熟青豆仁 -------------- 40公克
牛肉 ------------------ 300公克	蔥末 -------------------- 2½大匙
熟筍 ------------------ 150公克	豆瓣醬 ------------------ 1大匙
洋菇 -------------------- 80公克	薑片 ---------------------- 4片

❶
- 油 -------------------- 1大匙
- 醬油、酒、水 -- 各2小匙
- 糖、太白粉 ----- 各1小匙

❷
- 高湯 -------------------- 2杯
- 味噌、醬油 ------ 各2大匙
- 白醋、辣油、麻油 --------
  ------------------------ 各1大匙
- 糖、酒 ------------ 各2小匙
- 鹽、花椒粉 ------ 各½小匙

❸
- 水 -------------------- 1⅓大匙
- 太白粉 ------------- 2小匙

1 牛肉逆紋切片，入 **❶** 料拌醃，熟筍、洋菇亦切片備用。

2 鍋熱入油2大匙燒熱，入蔥、薑及豆瓣醬爆香，續入牛肉炒至肉變色，再入熟筍、洋菇及 **❷** 料煮開，最後入青豆仁及 **❸** 料芶芡盛起。

3 麵條置於盤上，淋上 **2** 項之材料拌勻即可供食。

880g.(2lb.) --- boiled plain noodle
300g.(10½oz.) -- beef fillet
150g.(5⅓oz.) ------ canned bamboo shoot
80g.(2⅘oz.) --- mushroom

40g.(1⅖oz.) - boiled green peas
2½T. minced green onion
1T. --------- soy bean paste
4 slices --------------- ginger

❶
- 1T. oil
- 2 t.each soy sauce, cooking wine, water
- 1 t.each corn starch, sugar

❸
- 1⅓T.water
- 2t.corn starch

❷
- 2C.stock
- 2T. each miso, soy sauce
- 1T.each sesame oil , chili oil, white vinegar
- 2 t. each , cooking wine , sugar
- ½t. each Szechwan pepper powder, salt

1 Slice beef against the grain, marinate in **❶**. Slice bamboo shoot and mushroom.

2 Heat the wok, add 2T. oil; stir fry green onion, ginger, and soy bean paste until fragrant. Add in beef, stir fry until color changes; add in bamboo, mushroom, and **❷**, bring to boil. Then add in green peas and thicken with **❸**. Remove.

3 Place noodle on a plate, pour sauce over noodle. Mix well before serving.

擔擔麵 • *Dan Dan Noodle*

熟陽春麵 ----------- 880公克　　榨菜末 -------------------- 2大匙
小白菜 -------------- 200公克　　花生粉 ----------------- 1⅓大匙
蔥末 -------------------- 3¾大匙

❶
┌ 高湯 ----------------- 6大匙
│ 芝麻醬 -------------- 4大匙
│ 鎮江醋、麻油 各2⅔大匙
│ 醬油 ----------------- 2大匙
│ 蒜泥 -------------- 1⅓大匙
└ 糖、花椒粉 ----- 各2小匙

1 **❶**料調勻成調味汁，小白菜洗淨切3公分長段，入開水中燙熟備用。
2 麵條置於盤上，上置小白菜，再淋上 **❶** 料並灑上蔥末、榨菜末及花生粉拌勻即可供食。

880g.(2lb.) ---boiled plain noodle　　2T. --------- minced pickled mustard head
200g.(7oz.) baby cabbage　　1⅓T. ------ peanut powder
3¾T. minced green onion

❶
┌ •6T.stock
│ •4T.sesame paste
│ •2⅔T.each brown vinegar, sesame oil
│ •2T.soy sauce
│ •1⅓T.garlic paste
└ •2t.each Szechwan pepper powder, sugar

1 Mix well all ingredients in **❶** to sauce. Wash baby cabbage and cut into 3 cm long sections; boil in boiling water until cooked.
2 Place noodle on a platter, top with baby cabbage. Pour sauce over; sprinkle on green onion, pickled mustard head, and peanut powder. Serve.

炸醬麵 • *Meat Sauce Noodle with Soy Bean Paste*

熟陽春麵	880公克	絞肉	450公克
胡蘿蔔絲、小黃瓜絲		蒜末	5大匙
	各200公克	麻油	1大匙

1[豆瓣醬、辣豆瓣醬、甜麵
醬 各2大匙

1 鍋熱入油5大匙燒熱，入蒜末、絞肉炒熟，隨入**1**料炒香，再加水2杯煮開，改小火燜煮至濃稠約10分鐘，再灑上麻油即為炸醬。

2 麵條置於盤上，排上胡蘿蔔、小黃瓜，再淋上炸醬拌勻即可。

880g.(2lb.) --- boiled plain noodle
450g.(1lb.) -- minced pork

200g.(7oz.)each shredded carrot,shredded cucumber
5T. ---------- minced garlic
1T. -------------- sesame oil

1[•2T.each soy bean paste, hot soy
bean paste, sweet soy bean paste

1 Heat the wok, add 5T. oil; stir fry garlic and pork until cooked. Add in **1**, fry until well mixed, then add in 2C. water and bring to boil, turn to low heat, simmer until sauce thickened (about 10 minutes). Sprinkle on sesame oil to be the meat sauce.

2 Place noodle on a plate, arrange carrot and cucumber on top. Pour sauce over, mix well before serving.

四人份　**serve 4**

麻醬麵 • *Sesame Sauce Noodle*

熟陽春麵	880公克
小白菜	200公克

1[熱高湯 6大匙
芝麻醬、麻油 --各4大匙
醬油、蔥末 ---各3⅓大匙
糖 2小匙
味精 ½小匙

1 小白菜洗淨切段，燙熟撈起，**1**料攪拌至糖溶化即為麻醬汁。

2 麵條置於盤上，排上小白菜，再淋上麻醬汁拌勻即可。

880g.(2lb.) --- boiled plain noodle
200g.(7oz.) baby cabbage

1[•6T.hot stock
•4T.each sesame paste, sesame oil
•3⅓T.each soy sauce, minced green onion
•2t.sugar

1 Wash cabbage, cut into serving sections; boil until cooked. Mix well **1** until sugar dissolved, this is sesame sauce.

2 Place noodle on a plate, arrange cabbage on top; pour sauce over. serve.

　四人份　**serve 4**

酸辣麵 •*Sour Spicy Noodle*

熟陽春麵 ----------- 880公克　　小白菜 ------------- 200公克

1 ⌈ 辣油、鎮江醋 -- 各4大匙　　**2** ⌈ 蔥末 -------------- 3¾大匙
　　│ 醬油 ----------------- 2大匙　　　　└ 榨菜末、蒜泥 -- 各2大匙
　　│ 花椒粉 ------------- 2小匙
　　└ 味精 ----------------- ½小匙

1 小白菜入開水川燙瀝乾，**1** 料與 **2** 料攪拌均勻即為酸辣汁。
2 麵條置於碗中，排上小白菜，再淋上酸辣汁拌勻即可供食。
■ 酸辣菠菜麵：將熟陽春麵改為熟菠菜麵，其餘材料及做法同酸辣麵。

880g.(2lb.) ---boiled plain noodle　　200g.(7oz.) baby cabbage

1 ⌈ •4T.each chili oil, brown vinegar
　　│ •2T.soy sauce
　　└ •2t.Szechwan pepper powder

2 ⌈ •3¾T.minced green onion
　　└ •2T.each minced pickled mustard head, garlic paste

1 Boil cabbage in boiling water until cooked, drain. Mix well **1** and **2** to be the sour spicy sauce.
2 Place noodle in individual bowls, arrange cabbage on top; pour sauce over. Mix well before serving.
■ Sour Spicy Spinach Noodle : Replace boiled plain noodle with boiled spinach noodle. The rest of materials and methods are the same as above.

四人份　**serve 4**

蔥開拌麵 •*Green Onion Sauce Noodle*

熟陽春麵 ----------- 880公克　　蝦米 -------------------- 60公克
蔥 -------------------- 240公克

1 ⌈ 水 ------------------ 3大匙　　**2** ⌈ 醬油 ---------------- 2大匙
　　└ 酒 ------------------ 1⅓大匙　　　　└ 味精 ---------------- ½小匙

1 蝦米洗淨，入**1**料蒸10分鐘，蔥洗淨切段，蔥白、蔥綠分開。
2 鍋熱入油5大匙燒熱，入蝦米炒香，再入蔥白炒至淺褐色，再入
　　2 料及蔥綠拌勻即為蔥油料，淋在麵條上拌勻即可。
■ 喜好洋蔥口味者可以洋蔥丁取代蔥段。

880g.(2lb.) -----boild plain noodle
240g.(8²/₅oz.) green onion　　60g.(2¹/₉oz.) ---dried baby shrimp

1 ⌈ •3T.water　　　　**2** •2T.soy sauce
　　└ •1⅓T.cooking wine

1 Wash clean dried baby shrimp, mix in **1** and steam for 10 minutes. Wash green onion clean and cut into sections, divide green and white sections.
2 Heat the wok, add 5T. oil and heat to hot; stir fry dried baby shrimp until fragrant. Add in white sections to fry until light brown. Stir in green sections and season with **2**, mix well to be green onion sauce. Pour over noodle and mix evenly. Serve.
■ Green onion can be replaced by minced onion depends on personal taste.

四人份　**serve 4**

雙絲拌麵・*Beef and Pepper Noodle*

熟陽春麵 ----------- 880公克	紅辣椒絲 ------------- 10公克
牛肉 ---------------- 300公克	蒜末 --------------------- 1大匙
青椒絲 ------------- 290公克	

1
- 蛋 ----------------------- ½個
- 油 ---------------------- 2大匙
- 醬油、水 ------ 各1⅓大匙
- 太白粉 -------------- 2小匙
- 糖 --------------------- 1小匙

2
- 水 ------------------------ ½杯
- 鹽、麻油 ------- 各1小匙
- 味精 ----------------- ½小匙

1 牛肉切絲入 **1** 料拌醃，鍋熱入油4大匙燒熱，爆香蒜末，續入牛肉炒熟，再入青椒、紅辣椒略炒，最後入 **2** 料煮開即為拌麵料。

2 麵條置於盤上，入拌麵料拌勻即可。

880g.(2lb.) --- boiled plain noodle
290g.(10⅕oz.) -- shredded green pepper

300g.(10½oz.) -------- beef
10g.(⅓oz.) ------- shredded red pepper
1T. --------- minced ginger

1
- ½ egg
- 2T.oil
- 1⅓T.each soy sauce, water
- 2t.corn starch
- 1t.sugar

2
- ½C.water
- 1t.each salt, sesame oil

1 Shred beef and marinate in **1**. Heat the wok, add 4T. oil and heat to hot; stir fry garlic until fragrant. Stir in beef and fry until cooked, then add in green pepper and red pepper to fry slightly. Pour in **2** and bring to boil to be the sauce.

2 Place noodle on a plate, mix well with the sauce and serve.

雞絲涼麵 · *Cold Chicken Noodle*

熟陽春麵 ----------- 880公克	綠豆芽 -------------- 100公克
雞胸肉 -------------- 200公克	鹽 ------------------------ ²/₃小匙
小黃瓜 -------------- 150公克	

1〔 蔥末 ----------------- 2大匙
  〔 薑泥、蒜泥 ------- 各²/₃大匙

2〔 冷高湯 ------------------- ½杯
  〔 醬油 ---------------- 3 ⅓大匙
  〔 芝麻醬、麻油 -- 各2大匙
  〔 辣油、糖、白醋各1大匙
  〔 花椒粉 -------------- ½小匙
  〔 鹽 --------------------- ⅓小匙
  〔 味精 ------------------- ¼小匙

1 雞胸肉入開水煮熟，取出待涼剝絲。
2 綠豆芽入開水中川燙後，以冷開水漂涼，小黃瓜切絲，加鹽醃10
　　分鐘後，洗去鹽分備用。
3 將綠豆芽置盤底，依序放上麵條、小黃瓜絲與雞絲，食時灑上 調
　　勻之 **1** 料，再淋上拌勻之 **2** 料即可。

880g.(2lb.) ----- boild plain noodle	150g.(5⅓oz.) --- cucumber
200g.(7oz.)chicken breast	100g.(3½oz.) bean sprout
	²/₃t. ----------------------- salt

1〔 •2T.minced green onion
  〔 •²/₃T.each ginger paste, garlic paste

2〔 •½C.cold stock
  〔 •3⅓T.soy sauce
  〔 •2T.each sesame oil, sesame paste
  〔 •1T.each chili oil, sugar, white vinegar
  〔 •½t.Szechwan pepper powder
  〔 •⅓t.salt

1 Cook chicken in boiling water until done. Shred by hand when cold.
2 Parboil bean sprout and rinse under cold water, drain. Shred cucumber, and marinate with salt for 10 minutes; wash off salt and pat dry.
3 Place bean sprout at the bottom of a plate, arrange noodle, cucumber, and chicken on top. Sprinkle on **1**, and pour well-mixed sauce **2**. Serve.

蝦仁冷麵 • *Cold Shrimp Noodle*

熟陽春麵 ----------- 880公克	太白粉 --------------------- 1 大匙
嫩薑絲 ----------------- 30公克	

1
- 蝦仁 ----------- 180公克
- 銀芽 ----------- 80公克
- 香菇 ----------- 10公克

2
- 麻油 ---------------- 1⅓大匙
- 糖 ---------------------- ½小匙

3
- 高湯、醬油、芝麻醬 ----- -------------------- 各2大匙
- 麻油 ----------------- 1 大匙
- 白醋、辣油 ------ 各2小匙
- 糖、味精 --------- 各½小匙
- 鹽 --------------------- ¼小匙

1 蝦仁洗淨加太白粉拌醃，香菇泡軟去蒂切絲，**1** 料均入開水中燙熟，嫩薑絲入 **2** 料拌醃30分鐘備用。
2 麵條置於盤上，**1** 料排於麵上，再灑上薑絲，淋上 **3** 料拌勻即可供食。
■ 蝦仁冷麵之熟陽春麵可以熟刀切麵取代。

880g.(2lb.) ---boiled plain noodle		30g.(1oz.) -------shredded young ginger
1T. --------------corn starch		

1
- 180g.(6oz.) shelled shrimp
- 80g.(2⁴/₅oz.) bean sprout
- 10g.(⅓oz.) dried black mushroom

2
- 1⅓T.sesame oil
- ½t.sugar

3
- 2T. each soy sauce , stock, sesame paste
- 1T. sesame oil
- 2t. each white vinegar, chili oil
- ½t.sugar
- ¼t.salt

1 Wash clean shrimp and mix with corn starch. Soften mushroom in warm water, discard stem and shred. Boil **1** in boiling water until cooked. Marinate ginger in **2** for 30 minutes.
2 Place noodle on a plate. Arrange **1** on top, sprinkle on ginger. Pour well-mixed **3** over noodle. Mix well before serving.
■ Boiled plain noodle can be replaced by boild handmade noodle.

芝麻蔬菜麵 · *Vegetable and Sesame Sauce Noodle*

熟陽春麵 ------------ ８８０公克
菠菜 ------------------ ４００公克
蔥末、榨菜末 ------- 各２½大匙

1
- 醬油、芝麻醬 -- 各２大匙
- 辣油、麻油 ----- 各１大匙
- 白醋 --------------- １½小匙
- 味精、蒜泥、酒、糖 -----
  --------------------- 各¼小匙
- 花椒粉 -------------- ⅛小匙

1 將 **1** 料與蔥末、榨菜末拌勻即為調味汁。
2 菠菜洗淨切３公分長段，入開水中川燙，撈起瀝乾。
3 麵條置於盤上，菠菜置其上，再淋上調味汁拌勻即可。

880g.(2lb.) --- boiled plain noodle
400g.(14oz.) ------ spinach

2½T.each -- minced green onion, minced pickled mustard head

1
- 2T.each soy sauce, sesame paste
- 1T.each chili oil, sesame oil
- 1½t.white vinegar
- ¼t.each garlic paste, sugar, cooking wine
- ⅛t.Szechwan pepper powder

1 Mix **1** with green onion, pickled mustard head well to be the seasoning sauce.
2 Wash spinach clean and cut into 3 cm long serving sections; cook in boiling water and drain.
3 Place noodle on a plate, arrange spinach on top; pour sauce over. Mix well before serving.

泡菜涼麵 • *Pickled Vegetable Noodle*

熟陽春麵----------- 880公克
榨菜絲、白蘿蔔絲、胡蘿蔔絲
--------------------各150公克
鹽 ----------------------- 1小匙

1 糖、白醋 -------- 各4大匙
醬油 ----------------- 2大匙
油、麻油 ------ 各1½大匙
芹菜末 ---------------- 1大匙

1 榨菜絲漂水去鹽分，白蘿蔔絲、胡蘿蔔絲入鹽拌醃後去水備用。
2 麵條置於盤上，上置 **1** 項之材料，再淋上 **1** 料拌勻即可供食。

880g.(2lb.) ---boiled plain noodle
150g.(5⅓oz)each ----------
shredded pickled mustard head, shredded turnip, shredded carrot
1t. -----------------------salt

1
•4T.each sugar, white vinegar
•2T.soy sauce
•1½T. each oil, sesame oil
•1T.minced celery

1 Rinse off salt in mustard head. Mix turnip and carrot with salt and pat dry.
2 Place noodle on a plate, arrange all vegetable on top; pour well-mixed sauce **1** over. Mix well before serving.

四人份　serve 4

家常涼麵 • *Home Favorite Cold Noodle*

熟陽春麵----------- 880公克

1
醬油 ------------- 4大匙
糖、芝麻醬 ----- 各2大匙
白醋 ---------------- 1大匙
麻油、辣油 ----- 各2小匙
味精 ---------------- ¼小匙

2
豬腿肉 -------- 200公克
花枝淨重 ----- 100公克
小黃瓜絲 -------- 70公克
蔥末、薑末------ 各¾大匙
蛋 ---------------------- 2個

1 豬腿肉、花枝入開水煮熟後切絲，蛋打散煎成蛋皮亦切絲。
2 麵條置於盤上，**2** 料排於麵上，再淋上拌勻之 **1** 料即可。

880g.(2lb.) ---boiled plain noodle

1
•4T.soy sauce
•2T.each sugar, sesame paste
•1T white vinegar
•2t.each sesame oil, chili oil

2
•200g.(7oz.)pork hind leg
•100g.(3½oz.)squid, net weight
•70g.(2½oz.)shredded cucumber
•¾T.each minced green onion, minced ginger
•2 eggs

1 Boil pork and squid in boiling water until cooked; shred. Beat eggs and make egg crepes; shred.
2 Place noodle on a plate, arrange **2** neatly on top. Pour well-mixed sauce **1** over. Serve.

　四人份　serve 4

辣味涼麵 ・*Cold Spicy Noodle*

熟陽春麵 ---------- 880公克		醬油、辣油 ----- 各3大匙
榨菜 -------------- 200公克	**1**	麻油 ---------------- 2大匙
蔥末 --------------- 3¾大匙		酒、糖 ----------- 各½小匙
		味精、花椒粉 --- 各¼小匙

1 榨菜稍微泡水去鹽分，切末備用。
2 麵條置於盤上，灑上蔥末、榨菜末，食時淋上 **1** 料拌勻即可。

880g.(2lb.) --- boiled plain noodle		•3T.each soy sauce, chili oil
200g.(7oz.) ------- pickled mustard head	**1**	•2T.sesame oil
3¾T. minced green onion		•½t.each cooking wine, sugar
		•¼t.Szechwan pepper powder

1 Soak mustard head in water a while to rid the salt, mince.
2 Place noodle on a plate, sprinkle on green onion and mustard head. Pour well-mixed sauce **1** before serving.

四人份　**serve 4**

薑醋涼麵 ・ *Ginger and Vinegar Noodle*

熟陽春麵 ----------- 880公克

	雞胸肉 -------- 225公克		薑末、醬油 ----- 各4大匙	
1	豌豆莢、胡蘿蔔 ---------- ----------- 各160公克	**2**	烏醋、麻油 ----- 各2大匙	
	蛋 ---------------- 2個		白醋 -------------- 1⅓大匙	
			糖 ---------------- 2小匙	
			味精 -------------- ¼小匙	

1 雞胸肉入開水煮熟待涼剝絲，豌豆莢去老纖維入開水中燙熟，胡蘿蔔切絲，蛋煎成蛋皮亦切絲備用。
2 麵條置於盤上，上置 **1** 料，再淋上 **2** 料拌勻即可供食。

880g.(2lb.) --- boiled plain noodle

	•225g.(8oz.)chicken breast		•4T.each minced ginger, soy sauce
1	•160g.(5⅗oz.)each snow pea pod, carrot	**2**	•2T.each brown vinegar, sesame oil
	•2 eggs		•1⅓T.white vinegar
			•2t.sugar

1 Cook chicken breast in boiling water until done, shred by hand when cold. Discard tough fibers on snow pea pod, scald in boiling water. Shred carrot. Beat eggs and make thin egg crepes, shred.
2 Place noodle on a plate, arrange **1** on top; pour well-mixed sauce **2** over. Mix well before serving.

四人份　**serve 4**　　　**91**

紅油涼麵 · *Chili Szechwan Noodle*

熟陽春麵 ----------- 880公克	蔥末、薑末 ---------- 各1½大匙

❶
| 雞胸肉 ------- 225公克 |
| 綠豆芽、青花菜 ---------- |
| 　　　　各160公克 |
| 紅辣椒 ---------- 20公克 |
| 蛋 --------------------- 2個 |

❷
| 醬油 ---------------- 4大匙 |
| 辣油 ---------------- 2大匙 |
| 麻油、烏醋 ----- 各1大匙 |
| 糖 --------------------- 2小匙 |
| 味精 ------------------- ½小匙 |

1 雞胸肉入開水煮熟待涼剝絲，青花菜去老纖維切小朵，與綠豆芽均入開水川燙漂涼備用。

2 蛋打散煎成蛋皮，紅辣椒去籽，兩者均切絲。

3 麵條置於盤上，上置 ❶ 料，再淋上 ❷ 料並灑上蔥、薑末拌勻即可供食。

880g.(2lb.) ---boiled plain noodle

1½T.each --minced green onion , minced ginger

❶
- •225g.(8oz.) chicken breast
- •160g.(5³/₅oz.)each bean sprout, broccoli
- •20g.(²/₃oz.)red pepper
- •2 eggs

❷
- •4T.soy sauce
- •2T.chili oil
- •1T.each sesame oil, brown vinegar
- •2t.sugar

1 Cook chicken breast in boiling water until done, shred by hand when cold. Discard tough fibers of broccoli and cut into small sprigs; boil in boiling water with bean sprout, rinse under cold water and drain.

2 Beat eggs and make thin egg crepes, shred. Discard seeds in red pepper and shred.

3 Place noodle on a plate, arrange ❶ on top. Pour well-mixed sauce ❷ over, sprinkle on green onion and ginger. Mix well before serving.

椒麻涼麵 • *Szechwan Pepper Sauce Noodle*

熟陽春麵 ----------- ８８０公克	蔥末、薑末 ----------- 各¾大匙
太白粉 -------------------- 1 大匙	

1 ⎰ 小黃瓜 ------- ３００公克
蝦仁 ----------- ２２５公克
熟筍 ----------- １００公克
紅辣椒 ---------- ２０公克
蛋 ------------------- 3 個

2 ⎰ 醬油 ----------------- 4 大匙
麻油、烏醋、辣油 --------
------------------- 各 1 大匙
糖 -------------------- 2 小匙
花椒粉、味精 --- 各½小匙

1 蝦仁洗淨加太白粉拌醃後，入開水中燙熟，小黃瓜、筍、紅辣椒均切絲，蛋打散煎成蛋皮切絲。

2 麵條置於盤上，**1** 料排於麵上，再灑上蔥、薑末，食時淋上**2**料拌勻即可供食。

■**1** 料可依個人喜好而變更。

880g.(2lb.) ---------- boiled plain noodle
1T. ------------- corn starch

¾T.each ---- minced green onion, minced ginger

1 ⎰ •300g.(10½oz.) cucumber
•225g.(8oz.) shelled shrimp
•100g.(3½oz.) boiled bamboo shoot
•20g.(⅔oz.) red pepper
•3 eggs

2 ⎰ •4T.soy sauce
•1T.each sesame oil, brown vinegar, chili oil
•2t.sugar
•½t.Szechwan pepper powder

1 Wash shrimp clean and marinate with corn starch; cook in boiling water until done. Shred cucumber, bamboo, and red pepper. Beat eggs and make thin egg crepes; shred.

2 Place noodle on a plate, arrange all materials in **1** on top; sprinkle on green onion and ginger. Pour sauce **2** over before serving.

■ Materials in **1** can be altered according to personal taste.

味全

濃濃的味全珍味油膏

甘到底！

濃濃的味全珍味油膏

每一滴都是純豆麥釀造的醬中極品，

無論沾、煮、滷，

都能增加各式美食的絕色、芳香與美味！

試試看！你會發現

即使用到最後一滴，

味全珍味油膏依然不改甘醇本色，甘到底！

純靑食譜　傳遞溫馨

微波爐第一册
- ●62道菜
- ●112頁
- ●中英對照
- ●平裝250元
  精裝300元

微波爐第二册
- ●76道菜
- ●128頁
- ●中英對照
- ●平裝280元
  精裝330元

健康食譜
- ●100道菜
- ●120頁
- ●中英對照
- ●平裝250元

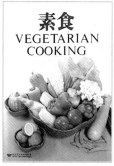

素食
- ●84道菜
- ●116頁
- ●中英對照
- ●平裝250元
  精裝300元

台灣菜
- ●73道菜
- ●120頁
- ●中英對照
- ●平裝280元
  精裝330元

四川菜
- ●115道菜
- ●96頁
- ●中英對照
- ●平裝250元

飲茶食譜
- ●88道菜
- ●128頁
- ●中英對照
- ●平裝300元
  精裝350元

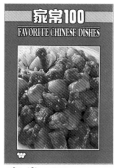

家常100
- ●100道菜
- ●96頁
- ●中英對照
- ●平裝250元

嬰幼兒食譜
- ●55道菜
- ●104頁
- ●中文版
- ●平裝220元

麵食精華篇
- ●87道菜
- ●96頁
- ●中英對照
- ●平裝250元

米食 傳統篇
- ●83年出版
- ●96頁
- ●中英對照
- ●平裝250元

米食 家常篇
- ●83年出版
- ●96頁
- ●中英對照
- ●平裝250元

純靑出版社
台北市松江路125號5樓
TEL：(02)5074902・5084331
劃撥帳號：12106299

THERMOS®

膳魔師 眞空燜燒鍋

日本酸素株式会社

安全 烹調美味・方便兼具省錢

規　　　　　格	KPA-2000	KPA-3000	KPA-4500	RPA-4500	KPA-6000
容　　　　　量	2.0公升	3.0公升	4.5公升	4.5公升	6.0公升
6 小 時 保 溫 能 力	54度以上	67度以上	71度以上	71度以上	73度以上

燜燒調理，方便不花錢，用膳魔師眞空燜燒鍋，可以節省約百分之八十的電費，瓦斯費，

因此您所購買的花費很快的就省回來了，好處多多、方便又省錢、建議您心動不如馬上行動。

膳魔師THERMOS眞空燜燒鍋是日本近年來，於烹調器具上最大的發明。

它使烹調成爲人人簡單易做的事，利用高眞空保溫原理

如焓燒般的把食物燜熟，沒有高壓，不必害怕爆炸，爲您烹調出原味營養的美食。

眞空斷熱調理鍋的調理方法

①把調理材料及調味品放入內鍋。

②內鍋及料理放在瓦斯爐或電磁爐上加熱至水滾。

③內鍋及料理放入外鍋內蓋好蓋子，就在不用電或瓦斯下調理又保溫。

④隨料理的種類，過了一般調理法所需時間後，即已煮熟料理，可以享用。

總代理：皇冠金屬工業股份有限公司

地址：台北市重慶北路四段191號2樓
電話：(02)8135313～7 FAX：8135337

百貨專櫃：太平洋ＳＯＧＯ　8Ｆ　　南西新光三越7Ｆ　　新光三越站前店9Ｆ　　大葉高島屋Ｂ1　　豐原太平洋7Ｆ
台中來來7Ｆ　　中友Ｂ棟地下一樓　　台南遠東百貨5Ｆ　　高雄大統7Ｆ　　大立伊勢丹8Ｆ　　高雄新光三越9Ｆ